AF589451

BEYOND THE ALGORITHM

Practical Machine Learning Strategies

Jane Onwuchekwa

Beyond The Algorithm: Practical Machine Learning Strategies

ISBN 978-2-9822070-2-8

A catalogue record of this book will be available from the National Library of Nigeria.

DEDICATION

To the data scientists who see beyond the numbers, finding meaning where others see complexity. Your passion for discovery, problem-solving, and innovation continues to shape the future of technology. To my mentors, peers, and the incredible data science community this journey would not be the same without your support and inspiration. May this book serve as a guide for those who strive to turn theory into impact, beyond the algorithm

.

TABLE OF CONTENTS

FOREWORD

In today's data-driven world, machine learning is no longer just an abstract concept confined to research papers and academic discussions. It has become a powerful tool driving innovation across industries—from healthcare and finance to e-commerce and entertainment. However, as any experienced data scientist knows, building effective machine learning systems goes far beyond selecting the right algorithm. Success lies in understanding the nuances of data, the challenges of deployment, and the strategies that bridge theory and real-world application.

Beyond the Algorithm: Practical Machine Learning Strategies is a timely and insightful guide that goes beyond textbook knowledge to address the practical realities of machine learning. This book delves into the challenges professionals face daily—how to handle messy data, optimize models for production, and navigate the trade-offs between accuracy, interpretability, and scalability. More importantly, it equips readers with the mindset needed to approach machine learning as both a science and an art.

As someone who has worked in the field of data science, I understand that the gap between theory and practice can often feel overwhelming. This book does an excellent job of closing that gap, providing not just technical insights but also strategic thinking to help practitioners make informed decisions. Whether you're an aspiring data scientist, a seasoned machine learning engineer, or a product leader seeking to integrate AI-driven solutions, this book offers valuable perspectives that will elevate your approach.

I highly recommend *Beyond the Algorithm* to anyone looking to deepen their understanding of machine learning beyond the surface level. It is a must-read for those who aim to build models that not only work but create real impact in the world.

PREFACE

Machine learning is more than just algorithms and mathematical models—it is a dynamic field that transforms industries, reshapes decision-making, and redefines human-machine interactions. While the technical foundations of AI are crucial, real-world success in machine learning requires a deep understanding of how models are built, deployed, and maintained in complex, ever-changing environments.

Beyond the Algorithm: Practical Machine Learning Strategies is designed to bridge the gap between theory and practice. This book explores not only how machine learning models work but also how they can be optimized, deployed at scale, and maintained over time. From handling bias and ethical concerns to implementing MLOps workflows, continuous learning, and scalable AI architectures, this book equips readers with the practical knowledge needed to build robust, real-world machine learning systems.

Whether you are a data scientist, machine learning engineer, product manager, or business leader, this book will help you navigate the challenges of deploying AI solutions that are both efficient and ethical. With insights drawn from real-world applications across industries, *Beyond the Algorithm* offers a hands-on guide to making AI work beyond just theory—ensuring that models not only perform well in controlled environments but also thrive in production.

As AI continues to evolve, so too must our approach to building and managing machine learning systems. This book is an invitation to go beyond the algorithms, embracing strategies that make AI practical, scalable, and responsible.

INTRODUCTION

Machine learning has transformed industries, reshaping how businesses operate and how decisions are made. From personalized recommendations and fraud detection to medical diagnostics and autonomous systems, AI-driven technologies are becoming indispensable. However, despite the breakthroughs in research, many organizations struggle with one crucial challenge—translating machine learning from theory into practice.

Building a model in a research environment is one thing; deploying and maintaining it in a real-world setting is another. Issues such as data drift, computational efficiency, ethical risks, and model interpretability often emerge after deployment, making it clear that developing an accurate model is just the beginning. Ensuring that these models remain efficient, scalable, and fair requires a deeper understanding of deployment strategies, infrastructure, and continuous monitoring.

Beyond the Algorithm: Practical Machine Learning Strategies bridges the gap between theoretical machine learning concepts and real-world applications. This book goes beyond building models to explore how AI systems can be deployed effectively, optimized for performance, and maintained over time. It provides actionable strategies for handling challenges like inference optimization, model degradation, bias mitigation, and AI governance.

This book is intended for data scientists, machine learning engineers, and AI product managers who are looking to enhance their ability to design and implement machine learning systems at scale. Whether you're deploying AI models in production, optimizing inference for real-time applications, or ensuring continuous learning in a changing environment, this book offers a comprehensive roadmap.

By the end of this journey, you'll have a deeper understanding of what it takes to build machine learning systems that are not only accurate but also robust, ethical, and adaptable to real-world complexities. It's time to move beyond the algorithm and master the art of building machine learning solutions that work in practice.

1

Understanding the Real-World Machine Learning Pipeline

Machine learning (ML) is commonly associated with sophisticated algorithms and mathematical models, but in reality, it is a comprehensive, iterative process that involves far more than just writing code. The real-world ML pipeline is an end-to-end workflow that spans problem definition, data collection, model development, deployment, and ongoing maintenance. Each stage is crucial to ensuring that an ML solution is effective, scalable, and aligned with business or research objectives.

The journey begins with problem definition, where stakeholders must clearly outline the goal of the ML system. This involves identifying the specific problem that needs solving, understanding the domain, and setting measurable objectives. Without a well-defined problem statement, even the most advanced ML models can fail to deliver meaningful results. A deep understanding of the business or application context is essential to ensure that the ML solution addresses real-world challenges rather than just optimizing a mathematical function.

Once the problem is well-defined, the next phase is data collection and preprocessing. ML models rely on high-quality data, making this step one of the most time-consuming and critical parts of the pipeline. Data may come from various sources, including databases, APIs, sensors, or manual inputs. However, raw data is rarely ready for immediate use. It often contains missing values, noise, duplicates, and inconsistencies that must be addressed through data cleaning and preprocessing techniques. Feature engineering, which involves selecting, transforming, and creating features, plays a significant role in improving model performance by highlighting relevant patterns and relationships within the data. Following data preparation, model selection and training take center stage. This involves choosing an appropriate algorithm based on the nature of the problem, such as classification, regression, clustering, or reinforcement learning. Experimentation is a key part of this process, requiring multiple iterations to fine-tune hyperparameters, optimize performance, and prevent overfitting or underfitting. Practitioners often use techniques like cross-validation, regularization, and ensemble learning to improve generalization and robustness. Tools such as TensorFlow, PyTorch, and Scikit-learn facilitate model development, but selecting the right model requires expertise, intuition, and continuous experimentation.

Model evaluation is an essential step to assess performance using metrics that align with business objectives. Accuracy, precision, recall, F1-score, and mean squared error are some common evaluation metrics, but the right choice depends on the specific problem. A high-performing model in a test environment does not always translate to success in production, making it necessary to evaluate the model's behavior under real-world conditions. Bias detection and fairness assessment are also critical, as ML models can inadvertently reinforce societal biases if trained on unbalanced or discriminatory datasets. Once a satisfactory model is developed, deployment follows, which presents its own set of challenges. Deploying an ML model involves integrating it into an existing system, ensuring it meets latency and scalability requirements, and providing APIs or user interfaces for access. Deployment strategies vary, with options including cloud services, edge computing, and containerized solutions like Docker and Kubernetes. Unlike traditional software, ML models require continuous monitoring because their performance can degrade over time due to data drift, changing patterns, or unforeseen edge cases.

Monitoring and maintenance are crucial in the post-deployment phase. ML models are not static; they require regular updates and retraining to remain effective. This involves tracking key performance indicators (KPIs), retraining with new data, and implementing feedback loops for continuous improvement. Model explainability and interpretability have also become important, especially in regulated industries where decisions made by ML models need to be transparent and justifiable. Beyond these technical aspects, successful ML implementation depends on collaboration between data scientists, engineers, domain experts, and business leaders. Communication and alignment across teams ensure that ML solutions address real-world needs rather than being purely academic exercises. Ethical considerations, such as data privacy, security, and fairness, must also be taken into account to build responsible and trustworthy ML systems.

Machine learning is far more than a collection of algorithms; it is a dynamic, iterative process that encompasses problem definition, data preprocessing, model training, deployment, and continuous monitoring. Success in ML requires a blend of technical expertise, domain knowledge, and a commitment to ongoing improvement. The complexity of the ML pipeline highlights the importance of a holistic approach, ensuring that ML solutions are not only technically sound but also practical, ethical, and aligned with real-world applications.

1. Defining the Problem and Setting Objectives

Every machine learning project begins with a fundamental step: defining the problem and setting clear objectives. This stage is crucial because it determines the direction of the entire project, guiding the selection of data, algorithms, and evaluation metrics. Without a well-articulated problem statement, even the most sophisticated machine learning models can fail to deliver meaningful results. The process of defining a problem is not just about stating what needs to be solved but also about understanding the underlying business or research context. It requires collaboration between data scientists, domain experts, and stakeholders to ensure that the ML solution aligns with practical needs rather than being a purely theoretical exercise.

The first step in problem definition is identifying the nature of the challenge. Machine learning is often applied to predictive analytics, classification tasks, recommendation systems, anomaly detection, and optimization problems. Understanding the category of the problem helps in selecting appropriate algorithms and methodologies. However, it is not enough to define the problem at a high level; the specifics matter. For instance, rather than saying, “We want to improve customer retention,” a clearer problem statement would be: “We aim to predict customer churn within the next three months based on past purchasing behavior and engagement metrics.” This specificity allows for measurable outcomes and clear paths to evaluation.

Another critical aspect of problem definition is assessing feasibility. Not every problem is well-suited for machine learning. It is important to determine whether sufficient historical data exists, whether the problem can be quantified, and whether an ML-based solution is the most efficient approach. Some problems might be better addressed with rule-based automation or statistical techniques rather than complex machine learning models. Feasibility studies involve exploration data analysis (EDA) to check for data availability, completeness, and quality. If data is inadequate, the project may require additional data collection efforts before proceeding.

Stakeholder alignment is equally important. Machine learning projects do not exist in isolation; they serve business or research goals that must be clearly defined from the outset. Engaging with business leaders, product managers, or clients ensures that the problem is framed correctly. Misalignment between technical teams and decision-makers can lead to wasted effort on models that do not address real-world concerns. For example, if an e-commerce company wants to optimize delivery times, the ML team must understand operational constraints, such as warehouse logistics, driver availability, and customer expectations, before designing a predictive model.

2. Establishing Clear and Measurable Objectives

Once the problem is well-defined, setting clear objectives becomes the next essential step. Objectives in machine learning should be specific, measurable, achievable, relevant, and time-bound (SMART). A vague goal like "improving product recommendations" does not provide enough direction. Instead, a well-structured objective would be: "Increase the click-through rate of product recommendations by 15% within six months using a collaborative filtering algorithm." Objectives should also be aligned with key performance indicators (KPIs).

Different ML problems require different evaluation metrics, and choosing the right one is vital for tracking progress. In a classification problem, accuracy, precision, recall, and F1-score might be relevant, while in a regression problem, mean squared error (MSE) or R-squared values are commonly used. For business-oriented applications, objectives often translate into financial or operational metrics, such as revenue growth, customer retention, or fraud detection rates.

Scalability and deployment considerations should also factor in objective setting. A model may perform well in a controlled environment but struggle when deployed at scale. Setting objectives that consider real-world constraints, such as computational resources, latency requirements, and integration with existing systems, ensures that the ML solution remains practical. For example, if an ML model is designed to provide real-time fraud detection for online transactions, it must operate within milliseconds to prevent delays in the payment process.

Ethical considerations and compliance requirements must also be integrated into objective setting. If an ML solution involves personal data, objectives should include data privacy, security measures, and fairness considerations. Regulatory compliance, such as GDPR or industry-specific guidelines, can impact how a model is developed and deployed. For example, a credit-scoring model must not only be accurate but also transparent and free from discriminatory biases.

3. Data Collection and Understanding

Data is the backbone of any machine learning model, and its quality directly determines the model's performance and reliability. Before any algorithm can be applied, an extensive data collection process must take place, ensuring that the right type of data is gathered from appropriate sources. Machine learning models learn patterns from historical data, meaning that the accuracy, completeness, and relevance of this data are crucial to achieving meaningful results. Poor data collection can lead to biased models, incorrect predictions, and ultimately, failed projects.

Data can come from various sources, including structured databases, unstructured text, images, IoT sensors, APIs, web scraping, and manual data entry. The choice of data source depends on the nature of the problem being solved. For instance, a recommendation system may rely on user interaction data from an e-commerce website, while a medical diagnosis model may need patient records and imaging data. However, merely collecting data is not enough—it must be relevant, diverse, and representative of the real-world scenarios where the model will be deployed.

During the data collection phase, several key considerations must be addressed:

i. Data Availability: Is there enough historical data to train the model effectively? If data is scarce, alternative methods such as data augmentation or synthetic data generation may be required.

ii. Data Quality: Is the data complete, accurate, and free of inconsistencies? Noisy or missing data can introduce errors into the model.

iii. Ethical and Legal Compliance: Does the data collection process comply with privacy laws such as GDPR or CCPA? Sensitive data must be handled with care, ensuring anonymization where necessary.

iv. Bias and Representativeness: Does the dataset fairly represent different groups, or does it suffer from selection bias? A biased dataset can lead to discriminatory model outputs.

Once data is collected, it must be stored securely and in a format that allows efficient processing. Data warehouses, cloud storage solutions, and databases such as SQL and NoSQL systems are commonly used for managing large-scale datasets. Accessibility is also a concern—data should be structured in a way that allows data scientists and engineers to retrieve and manipulate it easily.

4. Understanding Data: Cleaning, Exploration, and Feature Engineering

Once data is collected, the next critical step is understanding it through cleaning, exploration, and feature engineering. Raw data is rarely perfect, often containing inconsistencies such as missing values, duplicates, and outliers. Without proper data preparation, even the most advanced machine learning algorithms may struggle to produce meaningful results.

The data cleaning process involves:

- Handling Missing Data: Filling in gaps using techniques such as mean imputation, forward filling, or simply removing incomplete records.
- Removing Duplicates: Ensuring that redundant entries do not distort patterns in the dataset.
- Correcting Inconsistencies: Standardizing units, fixing typos, and ensuring uniform formatting for categorical data.
- Outlier Detection: Identifying and addressing extreme values that could skew model predictions.

After cleaning the data, exploratory data analysis (EDA) is performed to gain insights into its structure, distribution, and relationships between variables. EDA involves statistical summaries, visualizations, and correlation analysis to uncover hidden patterns. This step helps data scientists understand whether certain variables are highly correlated, whether there are imbalances in the dataset, and whether any preprocessing is required before modeling.

Feature engineering is another crucial part of data understanding. It involves selecting, transforming, or creating new features to improve model performance. Feature selection helps remove irrelevant or redundant variables, reducing dimensionality and improving efficiency. Feature transformation involves normalizing or scaling data to ensure that all variables contribute equally to the model. In some cases, domain expertise is required to create meaningful features that enhance the predictive power of the model.

For example, in a credit scoring model, rather than simply using raw numerical data such as income and age, additional engineered features such as income-to-debt ratio or average monthly spending can provide deeper insights. Feature engineering is often an iterative process, requiring continuous experimentation and refinement to optimize model performance.

Understanding data is not just about preparing it for machine learning models, it is about uncovering the story that the data tells. By thoroughly exploring and refining the dataset, data scientists can ensure that the final model is both accurate and interpretable, leading to reliable real-world applications.

5. Data Preparation and Processing

Raw data is rarely in a format that can be directly used in a machine learning model. It often contains missing values, inconsistencies, and noise that can negatively impact the model's ability to learn patterns effectively. Data preparation and preprocessing are essential steps that transform raw data into a structured, usable format, ensuring that the model can extract meaningful insights. These steps help eliminate errors, standardize data formats, and enhance model performance by improving both accuracy and generalization.

Handling missing values is one of the first tasks in data preprocessing. Datasets frequently have gaps due to incomplete data collection, system failures, or human errors. If left unaddressed, missing values can distort model training and lead to unreliable predictions. There are several approaches to dealing with missing data, depending on the severity and nature of the gaps. Simple methods include removing records with missing values, but this can reduce the dataset's size and lead to information loss. More sophisticated techniques involve imputation strategies, such as filling in missing values with the mean, median, or mode of the column, or using advanced techniques like predictive modeling, where missing values are estimated based on relationships with other features.

Another important step in data preparation is identifying and removing duplicate records. Duplicate entries can arise from data integration errors, multiple submissions, or technical issues in data collection. Keeping redundant records in the dataset can introduce bias and inflate the significance of certain data points, leading to skewed model predictions. Ensuring that the dataset contains only unique and relevant information helps maintain the integrity of the learning process. Data normalization and scaling are also crucial aspects of preprocessing, particularly when working with numerical features that span different ranges. Many machine learning algorithms, especially those that rely on gradient-based optimization, perform better when features are on similar scales. If one feature has values ranging from 1 to 1000 while another ranges from 0 to 1, the model may disproportionately prioritize the larger-scale feature. Normalization involves transforming data so that it follows a standard distribution, typically by rescaling values to a range between 0 and 1. Standardization, on the other hand, converts features to have a mean of zero and a standard deviation of one. Choosing the right scaling method depends on the specific algorithm being used and the characteristics of the dataset.

6. The Role of Feature Engineering in Enhancing Model Performance

Feature engineering is a critical part of data preprocessing that involves creating new features from existing ones to improve model performance. While raw data contains useful information, its true predictive power is often unlocked by carefully transforming and combining features in ways that highlight important patterns. This process requires domain expertise, creativity, and an understanding of how different variables interact within the dataset.

One common feature engineering technique is featuring transformation, where raw data is converted into more useful representations. For example, in financial data, converting a customer's total purchases into an average monthly spending metric can make patterns more interpretable. Similarly, in time-series data, creating lag variables or rolling averages can help capture trends and seasonality. Feature encoding is another important transformation, particularly when dealing with categorical variables. Machine learning models typically require numerical inputs, so categorical features must be converted using methods such as one-hot encoding, label encoding, or target encoding.

Feature selection is another crucial aspect of feature engineering. Not all features contribute equally to a model's predictive power and including irrelevant or redundant features can lead to overfitting and increased computational complexity. Feature selection techniques such as correlation analysis, mutual information, and tree-based importance scores help identify the most valuable attributes while eliminating unnecessary ones. In some cases, dimensionality reduction techniques like Principal Component Analysis (PCA) are used to compress high-dimensional data into a lower-dimensional space while retaining important information.

The effectiveness of feature engineering directly influences a model's ability to generalize to new data. Well-designed features can help capture hidden relationships that raw data alone may not reveal. However, poor feature engineering choices can introduce biases or overcomplicate the model, making it less interpretable and harder to maintain. Feature engineering is an iterative process, requiring continuous experimentation, validation, and refinement to ensure that the final set of features enhances model accuracy and robustness.

Data preparation and preprocessing are foundational steps in any machine learning pipeline. By handling missing values, removing duplicates, and normalizing or scaling features, data scientists ensure that the model can learn effectively. Feature engineering further refines the dataset by creating and selecting meaningful features that enhance predictive performance. These steps collectively reduce the risk of overfitting, improve generalization, and lead to more reliable machine learning models that perform well in real-world applications.

7. Model Selection and Training

Once the data is prepared, selecting the right model is a crucial step in the machine learning pipeline. This choice is guided by the nature of the problem at hand and the characteristics of the dataset. Different types of tasks require different approaches; for instance, classification problems, such as spam detection or medical diagnosis, involve categorizing data points into predefined classes, whereas regression problems, like predicting house prices or stock market trends, focus on estimating continuous values. Clustering, on the other hand, is used in unsupervised learning scenarios where the goal is to identify natural groupings in the data without predefined labels.

The decision to use a particular model is not solely about selecting the most sophisticated algorithm available. While deep neural networks and ensemble methods often produce state-of-the-art results in complex scenarios, they are not always the best choice. Simpler models, such as linear regression, logistic regression, or decision trees, can be more suitable in cases where interpretability and computational efficiency are priorities. A linear regression model, for example, is straightforward, easy to explain, and works well when there is a linear relationship between features and the target variable. Decision trees, on the other hand, are highly interpretable and can capture non-linear patterns but may be prone to overfitting if not properly regularized. The key is to find a balance between model complexity and interpretability, ensuring that the chosen approach is both effective and practical for deployment.

Once the model is selected, the next step is training, which involves exposing the algorithm to historical data so it can learn the underlying patterns. This requires splitting the dataset into training and validation subsets. The training set is used to teach the model by optimizing its internal parameters, while the validation set helps evaluate its generalization ability, preventing overfitting to the training data. Additionally, hyperparameter tuning plays a significant role in model performance. Unlike model parameters, which are learned during training, hyperparameters are predefined settings that control how the model learns, such as the learning rate in gradient-based algorithms or the depth of a decision tree. Various techniques, including grid search and Bayesian optimization, are used to fine-tune these hyperparameters for optimal results.

Model training is an iterative process that involves continuous refinement. After the initial training, performance metrics such as accuracy, precision, recall, and mean squared error are analyzed to assess how well the model is performing. If necessary, adjustments are made, such as modifying features, tuning hyperparameters further, or even selecting a different model altogether. The ultimate objective is to develop a model that generalizes well to unseen data, making accurate predictions while maintaining efficiency and interpretability.

8. Model Evaluation and Validation

Evaluating a model's performance is a critical step in the ML pipeline. Accuracy alone is often insufficient to assess a model's effectiveness, especially in imbalanced datasets or high-stakes applications. Metrics such as precision, recall, F1 score, and area under the ROC curve (AUC-ROC) provide a more nuanced understanding of model performance. Cross-validation techniques help ensure that the model generalizes well with unseen data. It is also important to validate the model against real-world scenarios, as performance on test data may not always translate to practical success.

9. Deployment and Integration

Deploying a machine learning model into a production environment is a significant milestone, but it is also one of the most challenging aspects of the ML pipeline. This phase involves integrating the model into existing systems, ensuring scalability, and addressing latency requirements. Deployment strategies vary depending on the use case, ranging from cloud-based APIs to edge computing solutions. Monitoring the model's performance in production is essential to detect issues such as data drift or degradation in accuracy over time.

10. Monitoring and Maintenance

The work does not end once the model is deployed. Real-world ML systems require continuous monitoring and maintenance to remain effective. This includes tracking key performance metrics, retraining the model with new data, and updating it to adapt to changing conditions. Failure to maintain the model can lead to a phenomenon known as "model decay," where the model's performance deteriorates over time. Proactive maintenance ensures that the ML solution continues to deliver value long after its initial deployment.

The Big Picture

Understanding the real-world machine learning (ML) pipeline goes beyond the mechanics of algorithms and mathematical models. It involves recognizing that ML is a systematic and practical approach to solving real-world problems, requiring a combination of technical expertise, domain knowledge, and business acumen. A well-structured ML pipeline ensures that data-driven solutions are not only accurate but also scalable, ethical, and aligned with organizational objectives.

The ML pipeline consists of multiple interconnected phases, each presenting unique challenges and opportunities. It begins with problem identification, where the objective is clearly defined based on business or research needs. This phase requires collaboration between data scientists, stakeholders, and domain experts to ensure that the problem is framed correctly. A poorly defined problem can lead to wasted resources, ineffective models, and solutions that fail to address real needs.

Once the problem is well understood, the next stage involves data collection and preprocessing. High-quality data is the foundation of any ML system, and gathering relevant, diverse, and unbiased data is crucial. Real-world data is often messy, requiring cleaning, transformation, and enrichment to make it suitable for model training. Data preprocessing, including handling missing values, removing inconsistencies, and normalizing features, ensures that the model can learn effectively. Additionally, exploratory data analysis (EDA) helps uncover patterns, trends, and potential biases in the dataset, guiding feature selection and engineering.

Model development follows as the next critical phase, involving algorithm selection, training, and optimization. Choosing the right model depends on various factors such as the problem type, data characteristics, and computational constraints. Model training is an iterative process, requiring hyperparameter tuning, regularization, and cross-validation to improve performance. The goal is to build a model that generalizes well to new data while avoiding overfitting. This phase also includes performance evaluation using appropriate metrics, ensuring that the model meets accuracy, fairness, and interpretability standards.

Delivering Impact Through Deployment and Continuous Improvement

Deploying an ML model into a real-world system is often more challenging than building the model itself. Successful deployment requires integrating the model into existing workflows, ensuring it runs efficiently in production environments and addressing scalability concerns. Infrastructure considerations, such as cloud computing, containerization, and API development, play a significant role in making ML solutions accessible and usable. Deployment is not a one-time process; continuous monitoring is necessary to track model performance, detect data drift, and make necessary updates.

Model maintenance is crucial for long-term success. Real-world conditions change, and a model that performs well today may degrade over time due to shifts in data distributions, evolving user behavior, or external factors. Regular retraining with fresh data ensures that the model remains relevant and effective. Monitoring tools help track key performance indicators (KPIs), flag anomalies, and automate the retraining process when necessary.

Beyond technical considerations, a holistic ML approach involves ethical responsibility and regulatory compliance. Bias detection, transparency, and fairness must be prioritized to prevent unintended consequences, particularly in sensitive applications such as healthcare, finance, and hiring. Ensuring explainability in ML models builds trust among users and stakeholders, making AI-driven decisions more interpretable and justifiable.

Mastering the end-to-end ML pipeline enables practitioners to move beyond theoretical algorithm development and deliver real-world solutions that create lasting impact. By balancing technical proficiency with domain expertise and business insight, ML professionals can build robust, scalable, and ethically sound systems that address complex challenges. The future of machine learning lies not just in optimizing models but in applying them thoughtfully to drive meaningful change in industries and society.

2

Data Preparation the Foundation of Practical ML

Data is the backbone of machine learning, forming the foundation upon which models are built and trained. No matter how advanced or sophisticated an algorithm is, its performance is entirely dependent on the quality of the data it learns from. If the data is flawed, incomplete, or biased, even the most powerful machine learning techniques will struggle to produce meaningful and reliable results. Real-world data, however, is rarely clean or structured in a way that allows models to learn effectively. It often comes from multiple sources, contains inconsistencies, and is filled with missing values, duplicate records, and irrelevant features. Without proper preparation, machine learning models may not only perform poorly but may also reinforce existing biases or make predictions that are misleading and unreliable.

Data preparation is a crucial process that ensures raw data is transformed into a structured, clean, and meaningful format before it is used for model training. This process involves several key stages, including data cleaning, preprocessing, and feature engineering. Each of these steps plays a vital role in optimizing the data for learning, improving model performance, and ensuring that predictions are interpretable and actionable. Data cleaning focuses on identifying and addressing errors in the dataset, such as missing values, duplicates, and outliers. Preprocessing involves normalizing or scaling numerical features, encoding categorical variables, and handling imbalanced data. Feature engineering enhances the predictive power of the dataset by creating new, meaningful features from existing ones, allowing models to capture deeper patterns and relationships.

One of the most significant advantages of thorough data preparation is its impact on model performance and generalization. Machine learning models are designed to learn patterns from historical data and apply them to new, unseen data. If the training data is not representative of real-world conditions, the model will struggle to generalize, leading to inaccurate predictions and poor performance on unseen examples. Well-prepared data reduces noise, removes inconsistencies, and ensures that the model learns from high-quality inputs. This not only improves accuracy but also enhances the stability and robustness of the model when deployed in real-world applications.

Beyond technical performance, data preparation also plays a critical role in making machine learning models more interpretable and trustworthy. In many business and scientific applications, decision-makers rely on AI-driven insights to guide strategic choices. If a model's predictions are difficult to understand or explain, stakeholders may hesitate to adopt the technology. By ensuring that the data is structured in a meaningful way, machine learning practitioners can build models that produce clear, interpretable, and justifiable predictions. This is particularly important in high-stakes fields such as healthcare, finance, and law, where AI-driven decisions can have significant consequences.

Despite its importance, data preparation is often overlooked in favor of more glamorous aspects of machine learning, such as model selection and optimization. Many beginners and even some experienced practitioners spend considerable time fine-tuning hyperparameters or testing different algorithms, while neglecting the quality of the dataset itself. However, experienced data scientists understand that well-prepared data often eliminates the need for overly complex modeling techniques. A clean, well-structured dataset allows even simple models to perform exceptionally well, while a poorly prepared dataset can cause even the most advanced algorithms to fail.

In the end, data preparation is what separates effective machine learning solutions from ineffective ones. It is not merely a preliminary step but an essential part of the entire machine learning pipeline. Organizations that invest time and resources into data preparation gain a competitive advantage by ensuring that their models are accurate, reliable, and fair. Machine learning practitioners who prioritize data quality over model complexity often achieve better results, as high-quality data allows models to learn more effectively and make more meaningful predictions. By focusing on thorough data cleaning, thoughtful preprocessing, and intelligent feature engineering, data scientists lay the groundwork for successful machine learning applications that drive real-world impact.

Data Cleaning: Eliminating Errors and Inconsistencies

Data cleaning is the foundational step in data preparation, ensuring that raw data is free from errors, inconsistencies, and inaccuracies before it is used for model training. Since data is often collected from multiple sources such as databases, web scraping, IoT sensors, and manual data entry, it is prone to various issues, including missing values, duplicate records, and outliers. These issues, if left unaddressed, can lead to biased or unreliable machine learning models. By implementing systematic cleaning techniques, data scientists can improve data quality, enhance model accuracy, and ensure that predictions are both meaningful and reliable.

One of the most prevalent problems in data cleaning is missing values. Data can be incomplete for several reasons, including technical malfunctions, human error during data entry, or limitations in the data collection process. If missing values are ignored, they can introduce bias or reduce the predictive power of a model, making it essential to handle them appropriately. One straightforward approach to managing missing values is removing records with excessive missing data. If a record contains too many missing entries, it may provide little to no useful information and can negatively impact the learning process. However, deleting too many records may lead to data loss, which can affect model generalization. Another effective method is imputing missing values, where missing entries are estimated rather than removed. Simple techniques include replacing missing values with the mean, median, or mode of the column. While these methods work well for numerical and categorical data, they do not always capture complex relationships within the dataset. More advanced imputation techniques, such as regression models or k-nearest neighbors (KNN), can provide better estimations by using the relationships between existing data points to predict missing values. In some cases, domain knowledge is required to determine the most appropriate way to handle missing data. Experts familiar with the dataset can provide insights into why values are missing and suggest meaningful substitutions or adjustments that align with the real-world context.

Another common issue in data cleaning is duplicate records, which can arise when datasets from multiple sources are merged or when data collection systems inadvertently store the same observations multiple times. If duplicates are not removed, they can skew the results of a model by giving disproportionate weight to certain records, leading to biased predictions. Detecting duplicates requires carefully examining the dataset for identical or nearly identical entries. While exact duplicates can be easily removed, partial duplicates may require additional preprocessing, such as fuzzy matching or deduplication algorithms, to identify and resolve inconsistencies. Ensuring that each observation in the dataset is unique prevents redundancy and maintains the integrity of the training data.

Outliers pose another significant challenge in data cleaning. These are extreme values that deviate substantially from the majority of data points. While some outliers are legitimate and provide valuable insights, others may result from errors in data entry, measurement inaccuracies, or corruption during data transmission. If not handled correctly, outliers can distort statistical analyses and negatively impact machine learning models, particularly those that rely on distance-based calculations, such as linear regression or clustering algorithms. Detecting outliers involves statistical techniques such as standard deviation, which identifies values that fall beyond a certain number of standard deviations from the mean, or the interquartile range (IQR), which highlights values that lie outside the expected range of the data distribution. More advanced methods, such as machine learning-based anomaly detection, leverage clustering or classification models to identify unusual data points based on their relationship to the overall dataset. Once outliers are identified, decisions must be made on how to handle them. In some cases, they should be removed if they are determined to be errors or irrelevant to the problem at hand. In other instances, particularly when outliers contain meaningful information, they may be adjusted or transformed using techniques like log scaling to reduce their impact while preserving their significance.

By carefully addressing issues such as missing values, duplicate records, and outliers, data cleaning ensures that machine learning models are trained on high-quality data. This step is crucial for building models that produce reliable and unbiased predictions, ultimately improving their real-world applicability and performance.

Data Preprocessing: Transforming Data into a Usable Format

After cleaning the dataset, the next step is data preprocessing. Many machine learning algorithms require data to be in a specific format, often numerical and standardized, before they can learn effectively. Data preprocessing involves transforming raw variables into formats suitable for modeling.

One crucial aspect of preprocessing is encoded categorical variables. Machine learning models typically work with numerical inputs, meaning that text-based categories must be converted into numerical representations. Common techniques include:

- One-hot encoding: Converts categorical variables into binary columns, where each category gets its own column with values of 0 or 1.
- Label encoding: Assigns numerical values to categorical labels, where each category is replaced with an integer.
- Target encoding: replaces categorical values with their mean target value in supervised learning problems, useful when there is a strong correlation between categories and the target variable.

Another important preprocessing step is scaling and normalization. Different features may have varying scales, which can negatively impact certain algorithms, particularly those that rely on distance calculations, such as k-nearest neighbors (KNN) and support vector machines (SVM). Scaling ensures that all features contribute equally to the learning process. The two most common techniques are:

- Standardization transforms data to have a meaning of zero and a standard deviation of one, ensuring that all variables are on a similar scale.

- Normalization: Rescales data to a fixed range, typically between 0 and 1, which is particularly useful for neural networks and gradient-based algorithms.

Handling imbalanced data is another key preprocessing step, especially in classification problems. If one class significantly outweighs another, the model may become biased toward the majority class. Techniques like oversampling the minority class, under sampling the majority class, or using synthetic data generation (such as SMOTE) to help balance the dataset and improve model fairness.

Feature Engineering: Enhancing Model Predictive Power

Feature engineering is a fundamental aspect of machine learning that significantly enhances a model's predictive capability by deriving new insights from raw data. While raw data contains essential information, it often requires transformation to fully capture the relationships between variables and improve model performance. By carefully designing new features through transformation, combination, or extraction, machine learning practitioners can boost model accuracy, reduce complexity, and improve interpretability. Effective feature engineering demands domain expertise, creativity, and a deep understanding of the underlying data, as well as how different features interact within a given problem domain.

A crucial aspect of feature engineering is featuring selection, which focuses on identifying the most relevant and informative features while removing those that introduce redundancy or noise. Not all features contribute equally to a model's performance, and some may even degrade its accuracy by adding unnecessary complexity. By selecting only the most important features, models become more efficient, interpretable, and generalizable. One widely used technique for feature selection is correlation analysis, which helps identify relationships between variables and eliminate those that are highly correlated. When two features are strongly correlated, they provide overlapping information, leading to redundancy that can negatively impact the model. By removing one of the correlated features, the dataset remains informative while avoiding unnecessary duplication.

Another method for feature selection is mutual information, which measures the dependency between variables to determine which features contain the most useful information for predicting the target variable. Unlike simple correlation measures, mutual information captures both linear and non-linear relationships, making it particularly valuable for complex datasets where interactions between variables are not straightforward. In addition, tree-based feature importance, commonly used in decision trees and ensemble models like Random Forests and Gradient Boosting, ranks features based on their contribution to model predictions. By analyzing how often a feature is used to split decision nodes and the resulting impact on predictive accuracy, this method provides an intuitive way to assess feature relevance and prioritize the most impactful variables.

Beyond feature selection, feature transformation plays a key role in improving data representation and enhancing model performance. Many datasets contain features with skewed distributions that can lead to poor generalization in machine learning models. For example, financial data often includes variables such as income, transaction amounts, or stock prices, which can have highly skewed distributions. Applying a log transformation to such features helps normalize the data, making patterns easier for models to learn. Additionally, polynomial features can be generated to capture non-linear relationships between variables. By adding squared or interaction terms, models can better understand intricate dependencies between features that a linear model might otherwise overlook. Another common transformation technique is binning, which converts continuous variables into categorical groups. For example, rather than using a customer's raw income as a feature, creating an income-to-expense ratio may provide a clearer indication of financial stability. Similarly, segmenting age into predefined ranges such as "young," "middle-aged," and "senior" allows for more structured and interpretable analyses.

Feature extraction, another powerful technique in feature engineering, involves deriving new meaningful features from raw data using domain knowledge and computational methods. In time-series data, extracting features such as rolling averages, time-based seasonality indicators, or lagged values helps models understand trends and patterns over time. For instance, in stock market prediction, a rolling average of stock prices over a specific window can provide a smoothed representation of price fluctuations, making it easier to detect upward or downward trends. In text analysis, natural language processing (NLP) techniques are instrumental in transforming unstructured textual data into meaningful numerical representations. Techniques such as word embeddings, which convert words into dense vector representations, enable machine learning models to capture semantic relationships between words. Similarly, term frequency-inverse document frequency (TF-IDF) assigns importance scores to words based on their frequency in a document relative to the entire dataset, allowing models to focus on the most informative terms while ignoring common but less meaningful words.

By strategically applying feature engineering techniques, machine learning practitioners can enhance model performance, improve interpretability, and make better use of available data. Well-engineered features help models learn more efficiently and generalize effectively to new data, ultimately leading to more accurate and reliable predictions across a wide range of applications.

The Impact of High-Quality Data Preparation

Data preparation is a foundational step that influences every stage of the machine learning pipeline. The quality and structure of data determine the effectiveness of the entire model-building process. High-quality data ensures that models are trained in reliable input, leading to more accurate and generalizable results. Conversely, poor data preparation can cause models to overfit, underperform, or produce misleading outcomes. In real-world machine learning applications, data is rarely available in a clean and structured format. Instead, it is often incomplete, inconsistent, and noisy. If these issues are not addressed adequately, they can significantly impact the model's performance, leading to unreliable predictions and flawed decision-making.

Proper data preparation involves multiple stages, including cleaning, preprocessing, and feature engineering, all of which contribute to creating a well-organized and meaningful dataset. The importance of these processes extends beyond just the technical aspects of machine learning. When data is properly structured and refined, models become more interpretable, which fosters trust among stakeholders and decision-makers. Transparency in machine learning is critical, particularly in business applications where organizations rely on AI-driven insights for strategic decision-making. Clear and well-defined features make it easier to understand how a model arrives at a particular prediction, reducing uncertainty and enhancing the credibility of the results.

Another significant aspect of data preparation is its role in ensuring fairness and ethical responsibility in machine learning models. Biases in training data can lead to unfair or discriminatory outcomes, particularly in applications such as hiring, credit scoring, or healthcare. If a dataset is not representative of the real-world population or contains historical biases, the resulting model may perpetuate or even amplify these biases. Addressing such issues requires careful examination of data distribution, balancing class representation, and removing any unwanted biases. Ensuring diversity and fairness in datasets is a crucial step toward building ethical and responsible AI systems that produce unbiased and equitable results.

Beyond ethical considerations, data preparation plays a key role in the scalability and efficiency of machine learning systems. Clean, well-prepared data enhances model training speed and reduces computational costs and improves overall performance. A dataset that has been properly normalized, encoded, and structured allows machine learning algorithms to converge more quickly and make better use of computational resources. Poorly prepared data, on the other hand, can introduce unnecessary complexity, making model training inefficient and increasing the risk of producing inaccurate results.

Ultimately, data preparation is what separates successful machine learning projects from those that fail. Organizations that invest time and effort into refining their datasets gain a competitive advantage by ensuring their models are robust, interpretable, and fair. Machine learning practitioners who prioritize data quality over complex modeling techniques often achieve better results, as even the most advanced algorithms cannot compensate for poorly structured data. By focusing on thorough data cleaning, careful preprocessing, and intelligent feature engineering, data scientists lay the groundwork for effective and scalable machine learning solutions that drive meaningful and reliable insights.

3

Choosing the Right Model for the Problem

The critical act of choosing the right machine learning model forms the bedrock of any successful machine learning solution. It's a decision that transcends mere algorithmic selection, demanding a nuanced understanding of the problem at hand and the characteristics of the dataset. Regardless of meticulous data preparation or the deployment of high-performance hardware, a poorly chosen model will inevitably lead to suboptimal outcomes, hindering the solution's effectiveness. Machine learning models, in their inherent diversity, exhibit variations in complexity, interpretability, and computational demands, necessitating a careful evaluation process.

The model selection process is not a pursuit of the most intricate or innovative algorithm but rather a quest for a model that achieves a delicate equilibrium between accuracy, efficiency, interpretability, and the crucial ability to generalize to unseen data. An inappropriate model can lead to the pitfalls of overfitting or underfitting. Overfitting occurs when a model becomes excessively tailored to the training data, capturing noise and idiosyncrasies that do not reflect underlying patterns, thereby compromising its performance on new, unseen data. Conversely, underfitting arises when a model is overly simplistic, failing to capture the essential complexities of the data, resulting in poor predictive capabilities.

Beyond the realm of pure performance, model selection carries significant practical implications. It directly impacts the feasibility of deployment, influencing factors such as computational resources, latency, and scalability. The choice of model also affects maintenance costs, as more complex models may require greater expertise and resources for upkeep and updates. Furthermore, in certain industries, particularly those subject to stringent regulations, model selection can have direct implications for compliance. For example, in healthcare or finance, the interpretability and explainability of the chosen model may be paramount for regulatory approval and ethical considerations.

A deep dive into the dataset is essential. Understanding the distribution of data, the types of features, the presence of outliers, and the relationships between variables are crucial steps. This analysis helps determine which models are likely to be suitable. For instance, if the data exhibits linear relationships, linear regression or support vector machines might be appropriate. If the data is highly non-linear, neural networks or tree-based models might be more suitable.

The nature of the problem itself also plays a vital role. Is it a classification problem, a regression problem, or a clustering problem? Each type of problem has its own set of suitable models. The desired outcome also matters. Do we prioritize accuracy, speed, or interpretability? For applications requiring real-time predictions, speed might be the most critical factor. In applications where understanding the decision-making process is essential, interpretability might take precedence.

Furthermore, validation techniques such as cross-validation are indispensable in evaluating model performance and preventing overfitting. By splitting the data into multiple folds and training and testing the model on different combinations of folds, we can obtain a more robust estimate of its performance. Hyperparameter tuning, the process of optimizing the model's parameters, is another critical step in maximizing performance. This involves systematically exploring different combinations of hyperparameters to find the optimal configuration.

In essence, model selection is a holistic process that requires a blend of technical expertise, domain knowledge, and practical considerations. It's an iterative process, often involving experimentation with multiple models and careful evaluation of their performance. The ultimate goal is to find a model that not only achieves high accuracy but also aligns with the specific requirements of the problem and the constraints of the application.

Understanding the Problem and Data Characteristics

The first and most crucial step in selecting a machine learning model is understanding the nature of the problem to be solved. Machine learning problems typically fall into categories such as classification, regression, clustering, and reinforcement learning. Each of these categories requires a distinct approach and model selection strategy.

For classification problems, the goal is to predict categorical outcomes. Examples include fraud detection, email spam classification, and disease diagnosis. Several models are suitable for classification tasks, including logistic regression, decision trees, random forests, support vector machines (SVMs), and deep learning classifiers such as convolutional neural networks (CNNs) and recurrent neural networks (RNNs). The choice among these models depends on various factors, including the complexity of the dataset, the need for interpretability, and the availability of data. Logistic regression is often used for simple binary classification problems, while decision trees provide a more interpretable structure. Random forests, which are ensembles of decision trees, offer improved performance by reducing overfitting. SVMs work well in cases where the decision boundary is complex and requires a hyperplane separation. In cases where large amounts of data are available, deep learning classifiers, such as those based on neural networks, can be highly effective, particularly in image and text classification tasks.

Regression problems, on the other hand, involve predicting continuous values rather than categorical labels. Examples include forecasting house prices, stock market trends, and predicting temperature changes. Common models for regression include linear regression, polynomial regression, decision trees, gradient boosting models (such as XGBoost and LightGBM), and neural networks. Linear regression is suitable when there is a strong linear relationship between independent variables and the target variable. However, when the relationship is nonlinear, polynomial regression or tree-based methods such as decision trees and gradient boosting become more useful. Gradient-boosting models, in particular, have gained popularity due to their ability to optimize performance by iteratively improving weak models. Neural networks, though computationally expensive, can capture complex patterns and are particularly useful when working with high-dimensional data.

Unsupervised learning problems, such as clustering, require models that can identify underlying patterns in unlabeled data. Clustering is a common unsupervised learning task that involves grouping similar objects based on shared characteristics. Some widely used clustering algorithms include K-means, DBSCAN (Density-Based Spatial Clustering of Applications with Noise), and hierarchical clustering. K-means is effective when the clusters are expected to be of similar sizes and are roughly spherical in shape. DBSCAN, on the other hand, is better suited for scenarios where clusters have varying densities and shapes, as it identifies high-density regions without requiring a predefined number of clusters. Hierarchical clustering provides a tree-like structure of nested clusters, which is useful for understanding relationships between data points at different levels of granularity.

Beyond categorizing the problem type, the nature of the dataset plays a crucial role in determining the appropriate model. If the dataset is small, simpler models such as linear regression, logistic regression, or decision trees tend to perform well because they require fewer data points for training. Deep learning models, on the other hand, are data-hungry and generally require large-scale datasets to achieve high performance. If the dataset contains a significant number of missing values or categorical variables, models that can handle such features effectively, such as gradient boosting methods, may be preferred. Decision trees and ensemble models like random forests and XGBoost, for example, can naturally handle missing values and categorical data, making them versatile choices.

The distribution of features in the dataset also has an impact on model selection. Linear models work best when the relationship between features and the target variable is linear. In contrast, tree-based models and neural networks can capture more complex, nonlinear relationships. If the dataset is imbalanced, meaning that one class is significantly underrepresented compared to others, certain techniques must be employed to ensure fair model performance. Tree-based models can handle imbalanced data effectively when combined with class weighting techniques, where the minority class is given more importance. Alternatively, oversampling techniques such as SMOTE (Synthetic Minority Oversampling Technique) can be used to generate synthetic samples for the minority class, while under sampling techniques reduce the number of samples in the majority class to achieve balance.

In addition to the dataset and problem type, computational efficiency and interpretability are also important considerations in model selection. Some models, such as deep learning architectures, require significant computational power and may not be practical for real-time applications or environments with limited resources. On the other hand, models such as logistic regression and decision trees are easier to interpret and explain, making them preferable in applications where transparency is crucial, such as healthcare and finance.

Ultimately, the process of selecting a machine learning model involves a combination of understanding the problem, analyzing the dataset, and considering practical constraints such as interpretability, computational efficiency, and the need for handling specific challenges like missing values or imbalanced classes. Experimentation and validation through techniques such as cross-validation and hyperparameter tuning are essential steps in finding the most effective model for a given problem.

Balancing Model Complexity and Interpretability

One of the most significant trade-offs in model selection is the balance between complexity and interpretability. Some machine learning models, such as linear regression and decision trees, are highly interpretable, making them suitable for applications where transparency is essential. In fields like finance, healthcare, and law, decision-makers need to understand why a model has made a particular prediction. Regulatory frameworks in these industries often require that machine learning decisions be explainable to ensure fairness and accountability. For instance, in credit scoring, a bank must be able to justify why a loan was approved or denied, which is why interpretable models such as logistic regression and decision trees are commonly used. Similarly, in medical diagnosis, doctors need to understand how an AI system arrived at a conclusion, making simple and interpretable models more preferable.

On the other hand, more complex models, such as deep learning and ensemble methods like random forests and gradient boosting, offer higher accuracy by capturing intricate patterns within the data. These models, however, function as "black boxes," meaning that their decision-making processes are difficult to interpret. While techniques such as SHAP (Shapley Additive Explanations) and LIME (Local Interpretable Model-Agnostic Explanations) can provide some level of insight into their predictions, they do not always offer the level of transparency required in regulated industries. Despite this limitation, deep learning models are invaluable in areas where raw predictive performance outweighs the need for interpretability. For example, in image recognition, natural language processing, and speech recognition, deep learning models such as convolutional neural networks (CNNs) and transformers consistently outperform traditional machine learning algorithms.

Another critical factor to consider in this trade-off is computational efficiency. Complex models require significantly more processing power and memory, which may not be practical for real-time applications or environments with limited computational resources.

Deep learning models, for example, require specialized hardware such as GPUs or TPUs to train and deploy efficiently. In contrast, simpler models like logistic regression or decision trees can run on standard CPUs and provide faster predictions. For applications like fraud detection, where real-time decisions are necessary, a deep learning model might be excessive if logistic regression can provide accurate results with lower computational costs. Conversely, in high-dimensional problems such as image classification or autonomous driving, traditional machine learning models are insufficient, and complex deep learning architectures are necessary to achieve the required performance.

Overfitting and underfitting are additional challenges that arise when balancing complexity. Overfitting occurs when a model learns the noise in the training data rather than the underlying patterns, leading to poor generalization on new data. This problem is particularly common in highly complex models, especially when the training dataset is small. Techniques such as cross-validation, regularization methods like L1 (Lasso) and L2 (Ridge) penalties, and dropout layers in neural networks help mitigate overfitting by preventing the model from relying too heavily on specific features. On the other hand, underfitting happens when a model is too simplistic to capture meaningful relationships in the data, leading to poor performance on both training and test sets. Linear regression, for example, may underperform when the relationship between features and the target variable is nonlinear. In such cases, more flexible models, such as polynomial regression or tree-based methods, are necessary to capture the underlying structure of the data.

Selecting the right level of complexity is crucial to achieving good generalization. If a model is too simple, it fails to learn essential patterns, resulting in underfitting. If it is too complex, it memorizes the training data instead of generalizing well to unseen data, leading to overfitting. The optimal choice depends on the specific problem, the amount of available data, and the computational resources at hand. Machine learning practitioners often experiment with multiple models, using techniques like hyperparameter tuning and feature engineering to strike the right balance between accuracy, interpretability, and efficiency.

Ultimately, the trade-off between complexity and interpretability is not a binary choice but a continuum. Some applications demand highly interpretable models, while others prioritize predictive performance. In many cases, hybrid approaches are used to leverage the strengths of both simple and complex models. For example, an interpretable model might be used for initial decision-making, while a more complex model is employed for deeper analysis. By carefully considering the problem context, dataset characteristics, and deployment constraints, machine learning practitioners can make informed decisions about model selection, ensuring that the chosen model is not only accurate but also practical and aligned with real-world needs.

Evaluating Model Performance and Optimization

Once a machine learning model has been selected, it must undergo rigorous evaluation to ensure its reliability and effectiveness in real-world applications. Model evaluation is not a one-size-fits-all process; different types of problems require different assessment techniques tailored to the nature of the task. Classification models, for example, are often evaluated based on their accuracy, but accuracy alone can be misleading, especially when dealing with imbalanced datasets where one class significantly outnumbers the other. In such cases, additional metrics provide a more comprehensive understanding of model performance.

Precision measures the proportion of correctly predicted positive instances out of all predicted positives, making it particularly important in scenarios where false positives carry high consequences, such as fraud detection or medical diagnoses. Recall, on the other hand, quantifies the proportion of actual positive instances that were correctly identified by the model, making it a critical metric for applications like disease screening, where missing a positive case could have severe consequences. The F1-score balances precision and recall, providing a single metric that considers both false positives and false negatives, making it useful when neither precision nor recall can be prioritized over the other. Additionally, the area under the receiver operating characteristic curve (AUC-ROC) evaluates the model's ability to distinguish between classes across different decision thresholds, offering insights into overall classification performance.

For regression models, which predict continuous values rather than categorical labels, different metrics are required. Mean squared error (MSE) measures the average squared differences between actual and predicted values, penalizing larger errors more heavily than smaller ones. Mean absolute error (MAE), by contrast, provides a more intuitive interpretation by calculating the average absolute difference between predictions and actual values. R-squared, or the coefficient of determination, quantifies how well the model explains the variance in the target variable, providing an overall measure of model fit. Selecting the appropriate evaluation metric depends on the specific objectives of the application. For instance, in financial forecasting, MAE may be preferred for its interpretability in terms of absolute monetary differences, while in scientific simulations, MSE might be more suitable due to its sensitivity to large deviations.

Beyond predictive accuracy, model evaluation also considers computational efficiency. Some models, such as linear regression and decision trees, are computationally lightweight and train quickly, making them ideal for large-scale applications with time constraints. These models require minimal computational resources and can be deployed efficiently, even on low-powered hardware. In contrast, deep learning models, particularly those involving neural networks with multiple layers, demand substantial computational power. Training such models on large datasets requires high-performance GPUs or distributed computing resources, making them more suited for tasks where achieving high accuracy justifies the additional computational expense. In real-world applications, striking a balance between accuracy and efficiency is crucial, as some use cases demand rapid predictions, while others prioritize highly accurate results regardless of computational costs.

Hyperparameter tuning is another critical step in model optimization, as many machine learning algorithms include parameters that must be fine-tuned to achieve optimal performance. These hyperparameters influence how the model learns from data and can significantly impact its effectiveness. For example, decision trees have hyperparameters such as tree depth and split criteria, which affect how detailed the model becomes in capturing patterns. Shallow trees may oversimplify the problem, while overly deep trees risk overfitting the training data. Support vector machines require selecting kernel functions that determine how the model maps input data into a higher-dimensional space to find a decision boundary. Neural networks have an even larger set of hyperparameters, including learning rates, activation functions, and the number of hidden layers, all of which shape how the network processes information and converges toward an optimal solution.

To systematically search for the best hyperparameter values, different tuning techniques are employed. The grid search exhaustively tests all possible combinations of predefined hyperparameter values, ensuring thorough optimization but at the cost of increased computational time. Random search, on the other hand, selects random combinations of hyperparameters, which can often yield near-optimal results while reducing computational burden. More advanced approaches, such as Bayesian optimization, use probabilistic models to intelligently explore the hyperparameter space, focusing on promising areas to find the best configuration more efficiently.

In many cases, even well-optimized single models may not perform optimally on their own. Ensemble methods enhance model performance by combining multiple models to create a more robust predictive system. One such technique is bagging, which trains multiple models independently on different subsets of the data and aggregates their predictions. Random forests, a popular bagging method, improve the performance of decision trees by training numerous trees on bootstrapped samples and averaging their outputs to reduce overfitting. Another powerful ensemble approach is boosting, which sequentially trains models so that each new iteration focuses on correcting the errors made by the previous one. Methods like XGBoost and LightGBM leverage boosting to build strong models that iteratively improve, making them highly effective for structured data applications.

By employing these evaluation techniques, computational efficiency considerations, hyperparameter tuning strategies, and ensemble methods, machine learning practitioners can refine their models to achieve optimal performance. Ensuring that models are both accurate and efficient while leveraging advanced optimization techniques allows for the development of reliable and scalable AI systems suited for real-world applications.

Selecting the Right Model for Long-Term Success

Model selection is a critical process that goes beyond simply achieving the highest accuracy on a given dataset. It is about identifying a model that will perform effectively in real-world applications while meeting various constraints such as scalability, efficiency, interpretability, and robustness to data distribution changes over time. A model that demonstrates high accuracy in an experimental setting but proves too slow, computationally expensive, or impractical to deploy in production loses its value.

Scalability is a major consideration in model selection, as the chosen model must be able to handle increasing amounts of data efficiently. In many applications, datasets grow over time, and a model that works well with small data volumes may become impractical as the data expands. For example, deep learning models, while powerful, often require significant computational resources, which may not be feasible in certain deployment environments. Simpler models such as linear regression, logistic regression, or decision trees might be preferable in cases where quick predictions are required and where computational efficiency is a key constraint.

Efficiency is another factor that plays a vital role, especially in real-time applications where rapid predictions are necessary. In scenarios such as fraud detection in financial transactions or autonomous driving, decisions must be made in milliseconds. If a model is too complex and slow, it becomes unusable regardless of its predictive power. Techniques such as model compression, pruning, and quantization are often employed to enhance the efficiency of complex models, but in some cases, simpler models may be chosen outright to meet performance requirements.

Interpretability is particularly important in industries where decision-making must be transparent and explainable. In healthcare, for instance, doctors and medical professionals need to understand why an AI model recommends a particular diagnosis or treatment plan. Similarly, in finance, regulatory compliance often mandates that organizations be able to justify automated decisions, such as credit approvals or fraud alerts. In such cases, models like logistic regression and decision trees are often preferred because they provide clear insights into how predictions are made. On the other hand, deep learning models, especially those based on neural networks, are often seen as "black boxes" and require additional techniques such as SHAP values, LIME (Local Interpretable Model-agnostic Explanations), or attention mechanisms to improve their interpretability.

Robustness to changes in data distribution is another key aspect of model selection. In dynamic environments where data patterns shift over time, a model must be capable of adapting without significant performance degradation. This phenomenon, known as concept drift, is common in fields such as e-commerce, where customer behavior evolves, or in cybersecurity, where new threats emerge continuously. Models must be monitored and updated regularly to maintain their effectiveness. Techniques such as online learning, retraining strategies, and ensemble methods can help improve a model's adaptability in such situations.

Beyond technical considerations, business constraints and regulatory requirements influence model selection. In many industries, legal frameworks dictate how machine learning models should function. For example, GDPR regulations in the European Union emphasize data privacy and explainability, requiring businesses to ensure their models do not discriminate against specific user groups. In contrast, applications like speech recognition, image recognition, and self-driving cars prioritize raw predictive performance over interpretability. In these cases, deep learning models, which may be less interpretable but offer superior performance, are often the preferred choice.

Model selection is not a one-time decision but an iterative process that involves continuous experimentation and refinement. Initially, multiple models are tested and compared using validation techniques such as cross-validation and performance metrics like accuracy, precision, recall, and F1-score. Hyperparameter tuning, feature engineering, and data preprocessing steps further influence the final choice. As new data becomes available, models must be reassessed and, if necessary, re-trained to ensure they remain effective.

By carefully analyzing the nature of the problem, understanding the dataset, balancing complexity with interpretability, and rigorously evaluating performance, machine learning practitioners can choose models that are not only accurate but also practical, scalable, and capable of solving real-world challenges effectively. The ultimate goal is to deploy models that add tangible value while maintaining efficiency, fairness, and adaptability to changing conditions.

4

Beyond Accuracy Evaluating Model Performance

Model evaluation is a crucial step in machine learning that extends far beyond simply measuring accuracy. While accuracy provides a basic measure of how often a model makes correct predictions, it is often insufficient for assessing real-world effectiveness. This is particularly true in cases where datasets are imbalanced, where different types of prediction errors carry unequal consequences, or where a high-stakes decision-making process demands more nuanced performance metrics.

A truly comprehensive evaluation of a model's performance involves multiple factors, including selecting appropriate metrics that align with the problem domain, understanding the trade-offs between different aspects of performance, and considering real-world constraints such as interpretability, computational efficiency, and robustness. Failing to properly evaluate a model can lead to misleading conclusions, poor generalization to new data, and suboptimal decision-making when deploying machine learning solutions in practical settings.

For instance, in applications such as fraud detection, medical diagnosis, and cybersecurity, a model that achieves high accuracy may still be ineffective if it fails to correctly identify rare but critical cases. If fraudulent transactions make up only 1% of the data, a model that always predicts "not fraud" would achieve 99% accuracy but provide no real value. Similarly, in medical applications, missing a disease diagnosis (false negative) can have far worse consequences than falsely identifying a healthy patient as sick (false positive). In such cases, accuracy alone fails to capture the model's true impact, necessitating alternative evaluation metrics such as precision, recall, and F1-score.

Beyond selecting the right performance metrics, model evaluation must also consider trade-offs between key factors such as bias and variance, precision and recall, and interpretability versus complexity. A model that is too simple may underfit the data, failing to capture meaningful patterns, whereas a highly complex model may overfit and perform poorly on new, unseen data. Similarly, in regulated industries such as healthcare and finance, a more interpretable model may be favored over a black-box deep learning model, even if the latter achieves slightly higher predictive accuracy.

Domain-specific considerations further complicate model evaluation. In autonomous driving, for example, models must be optimized for real-time decision-making and robustness against unpredictable conditions. In e-commerce recommendation systems, scalability and personalization matter more than absolute prediction accuracy. In finance, regulatory compliance and explainability are essential, requiring models that can justify their predictions with clear reasoning.

Ultimately, effective model evaluation requires a holistic approach that balances accuracy with other critical factors. By carefully selecting evaluation metrics, understanding trade-offs, and integrating domain-specific requirements, machine learning practitioners can ensure that their models not only perform well in experimental settings but also provide meaningful, reliable, and practical solutions in real-world applications.

1. Common Performance Metrics

Accuracy is the most basic metric, representing the proportion of correctly classified instances out of the total number of samples. While it is useful in balanced datasets where all classes are equally represented, it becomes misleading in imbalanced datasets. For example, in fraud detection, if fraudulent transactions account for only 1% of all transactions, a model that predicts "not fraud" for every instance will achieve 99% accuracy while being completely ineffective.

Precision, Recall, and F1-Score

For classification tasks, especially those involving imbalanced datasets, precision and recall provide a clearer understanding of model performance:

- Precision (positive predictive value) measures how many of the predicted positive instances are actually positive. It is crucial in applications where false positives are costly, such as spam detection, where mistakenly classifying a legitimate email as spam can cause inconvenience.

- Recall (sensitivity) measures how many of the actual positive instances were correctly predicted by the model. It is important in applications where missing a positive case is critical, such as in medical diagnosis, where failing to detect a disease can have severe consequences.

- F1-Score is the harmonic mean of precision and recall, providing a balanced measure when both false positives and false negatives need to be minimized.

ROC Curve and AUC (Area Under the Curve)

The Receiver Operating Characteristic (ROC) curve is a fundamental tool used to evaluate the performance of classification models, particularly in binary classification tasks. It provides a graphical representation of a model's ability to distinguish between positive and negative classes across different threshold values. The ROC curve plots the true positive rate (sensitivity) on the y-axis against the false positive rate (1 - specificity) on the x-axis, allowing for an assessment of the trade-offs between correctly identifying positive instances and mistakenly classifying negative instances as positives.

One of the key advantages of the ROC curve is that it evaluates a model's performance across all possible classification thresholds rather than relying on a single threshold value. This is particularly useful in scenarios where adjusting the decision threshold can impact the balance between sensitivity and specificity. For example, in medical diagnostics, a model used for cancer detection might be tuned to favor higher sensitivity to ensure that as many true cases as possible are identified, even if it results in some false positives. Conversely, in fraud detection, where false alarms can be costly and lead to unnecessary investigations, a model may be optimized to reduce false positives, even at the expense of missing some fraudulent cases.

The Area Under the Curve (AUC) is a numerical measure derived from the ROC curve that quantifies the overall effectiveness of a classification model. AUC values range from 0 to 1, where an AUC of 1 indicates a perfect model that can completely distinguish between positive and negative classes, while an AUC of 0.5 suggests that the model's performance is no better than random guessing. AUC is widely used because it provides a single value to compare different models, making it easier to determine which model has better discriminative power. A higher AUC means the model is more capable of correctly ranking positive instances higher than negative ones, regardless of the chosen threshold.

In real-world applications, the ROC curve and AUC are extensively used in domains such as credit risk assessment and medical screening tests. In credit risk modeling, financial institutions use classification models to distinguish between low-risk and high-risk borrowers. A high AUC value indicates that the model effectively differentiates between customers who are likely to repay loans and those who may default. This helps banks and lending institutions make informed decisions about approving or rejecting loan applications.

Similarly, in medical screening tests, the ROC curve plays a critical role in evaluating diagnostic models for diseases such as cancer, diabetes, and heart conditions. A diagnostic test with a high AUC ensures that the majority of diseased patients are correctly identified while minimizing false positives. For instance, in cancer detection, an AUC close to 1 means the model has strong predictive capability, making it a reliable tool for early diagnosis. Medical practitioners can use the ROC curve to determine the best threshold that balances sensitivity and specificity based on the clinical importance of false positives and false negatives.

Despite its advantages, the ROC curve is not always the ideal evaluation metric in cases where class imbalance is present. When one class significantly outweighs the other, Precision-Recall (PR) curves may provide a more informative assessment, as they focus specifically on the positive class. Additionally, AUC alone does not account for the actual distribution of predicted probabilities, meaning two models with the same AUC can have different practical implications depending on how their predictions are distributed.

Overall, the ROC curve and AUC are essential tools for assessing classification model performance, providing a comprehensive view of how well a model separates positive and negative cases across different decision thresholds. Their widespread use in fields such as finance, healthcare, and fraud detection highlights their effectiveness in guiding decision-making and optimizing machine learning models for real-world applications.

Logarithmic Loss (Log Loss)

Log loss is used in probabilistic classification models, where instead of just predicting a class label, the model assigns a probability to each possible class. It penalizes incorrect predictions based on the confidence level, meaning that a confident but incorrect prediction incurs a higher penalty than an uncertain incorrect prediction. This metric is often used in logistic regression and deep learning-based classifiers.

2. Trade-offs in Model Evaluation

The bias-variance trade-off is a fundamental consideration in model selection and evaluation.

- High Bias (Underfitting): A model with high bias oversimplifies the problem and fails to capture patterns in the data. For example, a linear regression model may fail to capture nonlinear relationships in a dataset, leading to poor predictions.

- High Variance (Overfitting): A model with high variance memorizes the training data instead of learning general patterns, leading to poor generalization on unseen data. Deep learning models, for instance, can overfit when trained on small datasets without regularization techniques.

Precision-Recall Trade-off

In many classification problems, there is a trade-off between precision and recall. Increasing precision often reduces recall and vice versa. The choice depends on the specific application:

- In medical diagnosis, recall is more important than precision because missing a disease diagnosis can have severe consequences.

- In spam detection, precision is more important because misclassifying a legitimate email as spam is more problematic than missing a few spam emails.

Computational Efficiency vs. Model Performance

Highly complex machine learning models often demand significant computational resources, making them impractical for scenarios that require real-time decision-making or deployment on edge devices with limited processing power. The trade-off between model complexity and computational efficiency plays a critical role in determining whether a model is suitable for a given application. While deep learning models with millions or even billions of parameters can achieve high predictive performance, their heavy computational requirements can pose challenges in environments where speed and efficiency are paramount.

One of the most prominent examples of real-time decision-making is in autonomous vehicles. Self-driving cars must process vast amounts of sensor data, including input from cameras, LiDAR, radar, and GPS, to make split-second driving decisions. In such an environment, there is no room for latency—delays in processing could mean the difference between avoiding an obstacle and causing a collision. Because of this, machine learning models deployed in self-driving cars must be lightweight and highly optimized for speed. Instead of relying on extremely deep neural networks, these systems often use a combination of compressed models, real-time data fusion techniques, and hardware accelerators such as GPUs or specialized AI chips like Tesla's Full Self-Driving (FSD) chip. The goal is to balance accuracy with computational efficiency so that decisions can be made within milliseconds, ensuring the vehicle operates safely in dynamic environments.

In contrast, large-scale recommendation systems used by platforms like Netflix, Amazon, and YouTube have more flexibility in terms of computational cost. These systems do not need to generate predictions instantly for every user interaction. Instead, they can afford to run complex deep learning models, such as transformer-based architectures, on high-performance cloud infrastructure. Recommendation engines analyze vast amounts of historical user data, behavior patterns, and content metadata to generate highly personalized suggestions. Since these computations are often performed offline or asynchronously, the need for ultra-fast, lightweight models is less critical. When a user logs into Netflix or Amazon, the recommendations they see are often precomputed or retrieved from a cache, minimizing the real-time computational burden.

Another key consideration in balancing model complexity and computational efficiency is deployment of edge devices. Many AI applications, such as mobile assistants, smart cameras, and IoT devices, require models to run directly on local hardware without relying on cloud-based servers. This is crucial for reducing latency, enhancing privacy, and ensuring functionality even in areas with limited internet connectivity. For example, facial recognition on smartphones must be fast and efficient, requiring models that are optimized to run on-device without draining battery life or overloading the processor. Techniques such as model pruning, quantization, and knowledge distillation help reduce the size and complexity of deep learning models while preserving their accuracy, making them suitable for deployment on constrained hardware.

The trade-off between computational efficiency and predictive performance is also evident in industries such as healthcare, where AI models are used for medical imaging analysis, patient diagnosis, and drug discovery. In hospital environments, real-time AI applications—such as automated anomaly detection in CT scans—must operate with minimal delay to assist doctors in making rapid diagnoses. However, in research-driven applications like drug discovery, where AI models analyze molecular structures and simulate chemical interactions, computational time is less of a constraint. In these cases, more complex models can be leveraged, often running on powerful supercomputers to process large datasets over extended periods.

Ultimately, the choice of model complexity depends on the specific requirements of the application. Real-time systems, including self-driving cars, robotics, and mobile applications, demand lightweight, efficient models that prioritize speed without sacrificing too much accuracy. In contrast, large-scale platforms with extensive computing resources can afford to use more sophisticated, computationally expensive models, as their predictions do not need to be generated instantaneously. Striking the right balance between accuracy, speed, and resource constraints is crucial for ensuring that machine learning models are both effective and practical in real-world scenarios.

3. Domain-Specific Considerations

In healthcare, models must prioritize sensitivity (recall) to avoid missing diagnoses. Additionally, explainability is crucial because doctors and medical professionals need to understand how predictions are made. Regulatory requirements, such as those imposed by the FDA, demand that AI-driven medical tools be interpretable and reliable.

Financial institutions use machine learning for credit scoring, fraud detection, and algorithmic trading. Here, precision is important to minimize false positives in fraud detection. Explainability is also necessary to comply with regulations that require transparency in decision-making processes, such as the European Union's General Data Protection Regulation (GDPR).

In recommendation systems such as those used by Amazon, Netflix, and Spotify, precision is often more critical than recall because these platforms aim to provide users with highly relevant suggestions that match their interests. A recommendation system with high precision ensures that the majority of suggested items, whether movies, products, or songs—are closely aligned with the user's preferences. This is essential for enhancing user satisfaction, increasing engagement, and driving revenue. If the system focuses too much on recall, it may retrieve a large number of items, but many of them could be irrelevant to the user's taste, leading to a poor user experience.

For instance, if Netflix's recommendation system suggests ten movies to a user who enjoys psychological thrillers, high precision would mean that most, if not all, of those movies belong to that genre and have characteristics that align with the user's past viewing habits. On the other hand, if the system prioritizes recall, it might recommend a mix of thrillers, horror movies, dramas, and action films simply because they share some metadata or are broadly popular. This dilutes the quality of recommendations, making it less likely that the user will engage with the suggested content. Similarly, on Spotify, if a user listens primarily to jazz, a high-precision system would recommend artists and songs that closely match the user's jazz preferences rather than throwing in a mix of pop and classical tracks just because they are somewhat related.

The impact of poor precision on recommendation systems extends beyond just user experience. When users are frequently shown irrelevant recommendations, they may lose trust in the system and engage with it less frequently. This can reduce retention rates and negatively affect business outcomes. Amazon, for example, relies heavily on its recommendation engine to drive product sales. If a user who frequently purchases organic skincare products is suddenly bombarded with recommendations for unrelated items like power tools or gaming accessories, they may start ignoring the suggestions altogether, reducing the likelihood of impulse purchases and negatively affecting conversion rates.

Scalability is another fundamental challenge in recommendation systems, as they must process vast amounts of data efficiently while maintaining high precision. Platforms like Amazon, Netflix, and Spotify deal with millions of users, each generating behavioral data in real time. These systems analyze vast datasets, including purchase history, watch history, search queries, and even subtle behavioral cues like how long a user hovers over a particular item before clicking away. Given the sheer volume of data, recommendation engines must be designed to provide real-time or near-real-time responses while maintaining computational efficiency. This is why many large-scale recommendation systems rely on machine learning techniques such as matrix factorization, deep learning, and graph-based models. Without proper scalability, the system may struggle to deliver timely recommendations, leading to delays that reduce the effectiveness of the recommendations.

In contrast, in cybersecurity applications, precision is equally, if not more, important than recall because of the need to manage alerts efficiently. Security systems use machine learning models to detect potential threats, such as unauthorized access, malware infections, and network intrusions. If a cybersecurity model prioritizes recall over precision, it may flag every possible anomaly as a potential threat, leading to a high rate of false positives. This can overwhelm security teams with excessive alerts, making it difficult to distinguish genuine threats from benign activities.

For example, an intrusion detection system monitoring network traffic might detect unusual activity patterns and flag them as potential attacks. If the system has low precision, it may generate alerts for harmless activities, such as an employee accessing a system from a new device or running an unfamiliar application. This phenomenon, known as "alert fatigue," can cause security analysts to become desensitized to warnings, increasing the likelihood that they will overlook a real attack when it occurs. In high-stakes environments, such as financial institutions or government networks, the consequences of missing a genuine security threat due to excessive false positives can be catastrophic, leading to data breaches, financial losses, and reputational damage.

A cybersecurity system with high precision ensures that when an alert is triggered, it is highly likely to be a legitimate security threat. This enables security teams to allocate their time and resources efficiently, focusing on real incidents rather than chasing down false alarms. However, achieving high precision in cybersecurity is challenging because cyber threats constantly evolve. Attackers use sophisticated techniques to bypass detection, requiring security models to be continuously updated and refined.

Balancing precision and recall in cybersecurity is crucial because an excessively high precision rate at the expense of recall might mean that some real threats go undetected. Security systems must find the right trade-off—minimizing false positives while still catching as many real threats as possible. To achieve this, modern cybersecurity solutions use adaptive machine learning models, anomaly detection algorithms, and behavioral analysis techniques to refine their detection capabilities.

Ultimately, while both precision and recall are important in machine learning applications, their relative importance depends on the specific use case. In recommendation systems, high precision ensures users receive relevant suggestions, improving engagement and conversion rates, while scalability ensures the system can function efficiently for millions of users. In cybersecurity, high precision helps security teams filter out false alarms and focus on real threats, reducing response times and improving overall security. In both domains, optimizing precision while maintaining an acceptable level of recall is crucial for building effective and efficient machine learning systems.

Model evaluation extends far beyond simple accuracy, requiring a nuanced approach that considers multiple performance metrics, trade-offs, and domain-specific requirements. While accuracy is often the most intuitive measure, it may not fully capture a model's effectiveness, especially in scenarios where class imbalances, rare events, or specific business constraints exist. The choice of evaluation metrics must align with the problem at hand, ensuring that the model performs well in practical applications rather than just achieving a high overall accuracy on a test dataset.

Precision and recall are two fundamental metrics that play a significant role in many applications, particularly those involving classification problems. Precision measures the proportion of positive predictions that are actually correct, making it crucial in scenarios where false positives carry significant consequences. For example, in cybersecurity, a model with low precision may generate excessive false alarms, overwhelming security analysts with unnecessary alerts. In contrast, recall measures the proportion of actual positive cases that the model correctly identifies, which is essential in applications where missing a true positive is costly. In medical diagnostics, for instance, a model with high recall is preferred because failing to detect a serious disease could have life-threatening consequences.

Beyond precision and recall, computational efficiency is another critical factor in model evaluation. Some models, such as deep learning networks, offer high predictive performance but require extensive computational resources. This trade-off becomes especially relevant in real-time applications where speed is a priority. A recommendation system that takes too long to generate suggestions loses its value, no matter how accurate its predictions are. Similarly, fraud detection models used in banking systems must process transactions within milliseconds to prevent unauthorized activities without disrupting legitimate customer transactions.

Interpretability is another key aspect of model evaluation, particularly in domains where understanding the reasoning behind predictions is necessary for trust and compliance. In regulated industries such as finance and healthcare, black-box models like deep neural networks may not be suitable because decision-makers need transparency in how a model arrives at its conclusions. Decision trees, logistic regression, and explainable AI techniques such as SHAP (Shapley Additive Explanations) and LIME (Local Interpretable Model-Agnostic Explanations) help bridge this gap by providing insights into model behavior. Without interpretability, even a highly accurate model may be rejected if users cannot trust their outputs or if regulatory bodies require explanations for each decision.

Scalability is another factor that determines a model's real-world applicability. A model that performs well on a small dataset may fail when deployed at scale. Social media platforms, for example, handle billions of interactions per day, requiring models that can maintain high performance under heavy loads. Similarly, machine learning models used in cloud services must be designed to scale dynamically as demand fluctuates. This requires careful consideration of model complexity, data storage requirements, and optimization techniques to ensure that predictions remain fast and reliable.

Effective model selection requires a deep understanding of the problem domain, continuous experimentation with multiple metrics, and iterative refinements based on real-world performance. Rather than relying solely on a single metric like accuracy, data scientists and engineers must evaluate trade-offs between precision, recall, computational efficiency, interpretability, and scalability to select the most appropriate model for their specific use case. This process involves running extensive validation tests, using cross-validation techniques to assess robustness, and monitoring the model's behavior in a production environment to detect potential performance drift over time. In many cases, hybrid approaches that combine different models or leverage ensemble learning techniques can help optimize multiple performance criteria simultaneously.

Ultimately, model evaluation is an ongoing process rather than a one-time decision. Real-world conditions change, data distributions evolve, and new challenges emerge, requiring continuous monitoring and refinement of machine learning models. By adopting a holistic approach that considers multiple evaluation metrics, businesses and researchers can ensure that their models remain effective, efficient, and aligned with the specific needs of their applications.

5

Handling Imbalanced and Noisy Data

Real-world datasets are rarely perfect. They often suffer from class imbalances, where one class is significantly more prevalent than others, and noise, which includes mislabeled data, missing values, and outliers. These imperfections pose significant challenges for machine learning models, leading to biased predictions, reduced generalization, and unreliable performance. Addressing these issues is crucial for building robust, fair, and effective machine learning systems. In this chapter, we will explore strategies to handle imbalanced and noisy data, ensuring that models learn effectively despite imperfections.

Understanding Imbalanced Data

Imbalanced data occurs when the distribution of different classes within a dataset is significantly skewed, meaning that some classes appear far more frequently than others. This imbalance is common in various real-world applications, particularly in domains where detecting rare events is crucial. Examples include fraud detection, where fraudulent transactions are significantly fewer than legitimate ones; rare disease diagnosis, where positive cases form a small fraction of the total medical records; and spam filtering, where spam emails make up only a portion of all received emails. In such scenarios, the dataset contains a dominant majority class and an underrepresented minority class.

The presence of imbalanced data poses challenges to traditional machine learning models, which are often designed under the assumption that classes are equally represented. When trained on imbalanced datasets, these models tend to become biased toward the majority class, leading to poor generalization for the minority class. This happens because machine learning algorithms, particularly those optimized using accuracy as the primary metric, naturally prioritize the most frequently occurring class. As a result, a model might achieve high accuracy by simply predicting the majority class in most cases, even though its performance on the minority class is poor. For example, in a dataset where fraudulent transactions account for only 1% of all transactions, a model that always predicts "not fraud" could still achieve 99% accuracy, despite being completely ineffective at identifying fraud.

The consequences of such bias can be severe, especially in critical applications. In fraud detection, failing to identify fraudulent transactions can lead to financial losses. In medical diagnosis, an incorrect classification of a rare disease as "negative" can delay treatment and have life-threatening consequences. In security applications such as anomaly detection, overlooking rare events might lead to undetected cyber threats. These examples highlight the need for techniques that can address class imbalance and improve the detection of minority class instances.

Several strategies can be used to mitigate the effects of imbalanced data and enhance model performance. One approach is resampling the dataset, which involves either oversampling the minority class by duplicating its instances or generating synthetic samples, or undersampling the majority class by removing some of its instances. Oversampling techniques such as SMOTE (Synthetic Minority Oversampling Technique) create synthetic data points that resemble existing minority class instances, helping the model learn more about the underrepresented category without excessively repeating the same data points. Undersampling, on the other hand, reduces the number of majority class instances to balance the dataset but runs the risk of discarding useful information.

Another approach is the use of cost-sensitive learning, where different misclassification penalties are assigned to different classes. In this method, misclassifying a minority class instance is penalized more heavily than misclassifying a majority class instance, forcing the model to pay more attention to the underrepresented class. Many machines learning algorithms, including decision trees, support vector machines, and neural networks, can be adapted to incorporate class-weighting mechanisms.

Alternative evaluation metrics are also essential when dealing with imbalanced data. Traditional accuracy is often misleading because it does not account for the distribution of classes. Metrics such as precision, recall, F1-score, and the area under the receiver operating characteristic (ROC-AUC) curve provide a more balanced view of model performance. Precision measures the proportion of correctly predicted positive instances among all predicted positives, while recall measures how many actual positive instances were correctly identified. The F1-score balances precision and recall, making it a useful metric in imbalanced classification tasks.

Ensemble learning techniques, such as bagging and boosting, also offer effective solutions for handling imbalanced datasets. Algorithms like random forests and gradient boosting machines (GBM) can incorporate sampling techniques or cost-sensitive learning to improve predictions on minority class instances. Additionally, deep learning models, particularly those using advanced architectures such as convolutional neural networks (CNNs) and recurrent neural networks (RNNs), can be designed with specific loss functions that emphasize learning from imbalanced data. Class imbalance is a prevalent challenge in machine learning applications where rare events must be detected with high accuracy. Traditional models trained on imbalanced datasets tend to favor the majority class, leading to poor performance in detecting the minority class. Addressing this issue requires specialized techniques such as resampling, cost-sensitive learning, alternative evaluation metrics, and ensemble methods. By adopting these strategies, models can be trained to recognize rare instances more effectively, leading to better decision-making in critical applications such as fraud detection, medical diagnosis, and cybersecurity.

Techniques for Handling Imbalanced Data

Oversampling the minority class is a widely used approach to address class imbalance in datasets by increasing the representation of the underrepresented class. One of the most popular techniques for achieving this is the Synthetic Minority Oversampling Technique (SMOTE). Instead of simply duplicating existing minority class instances, SMOTE generates synthetic samples by interpolating between existing ones. This helps prevent overfitting, a common issue when identical copies of minority class samples are repeatedly used for training. By introducing new, plausible instances into the dataset, SMOTE ensures that the model learns a more generalizable pattern of the minority class, improving its ability to make accurate predictions.

Another approach to handling class imbalance is undersampling the majority class, which involves reducing the number of instances in the dominant class to balance the dataset. This can be done randomly, by removing majority-class samples, or in a more sophisticated manner, by selecting the most informative instances while discarding redundant or less important ones. While undersampling can help in achieving class balance, it carries the risk of losing valuable information from the majority class, which can negatively impact model performance. To mitigate this, techniques such as NearMiss, which selects majority class instances that are closest to minority class samples, and Tomek Links, which remove instances that are easily confused with the minority class, are often employed to refine the dataset while maintaining crucial information.

Cost-sensitive learning is another effective strategy for dealing with imbalanced data by assigning different misclassification costs to different classes. In this approach, the cost of misclassifying a minority class instance is set higher than that of misclassifying a majority class instance, forcing the model to give more importance to correctly predicting the minority class. Many machine learning algorithms, such as decision trees, support vector machines, and neural networks, can be modified to incorporate cost-sensitive learning by adjusting class weights during training. This approach ensures that the model does not favor the majority class simply because it has more instances, leading to a more balanced prediction outcome.

Ensemble methods provide another powerful technique for handling imbalanced datasets by combining multiple weak models to form a stronger and more robust classifier. Bagging techniques, such as Random Forest, create multiple subsets of the training data and train different models on these subsets before aggregating their predictions. Boosting methods, like AdaBoost and Gradient Boosting Machines

(GBM), assign higher weights to misclassified instances, encouraging the model to focus on difficult-to-classify samples, which often belong to the minority class. An extension of boosting specifically designed for imbalanced data is Balanced Random Forest, which applies undersampling to each bootstrap sample to ensure balanced class representation during training. Another variation, Easy Ensemble, creates multiple balanced subsets from the majority class and trains separate classifiers on them, ultimately combining their predictions for improved performance.

Hybrid methods integrate both oversampling and undersampling techniques to achieve an optimal balance in the dataset. These approaches seek to mitigate the drawbacks of each individual method by intelligently resampling the data to maintain sufficient information while addressing class imbalance. One common hybrid approach is SMOTE combined with Tomek Links, where synthetic minority class instances are first generated using SMOTE, and then Tomek Links is applied to remove ambiguous majority class samples. This combination enhances the separation between the two classes and reduces noise in the dataset, leading to better classification performance.

Evaluation metrics play a critical role in assessing model performance on imbalanced datasets, as traditional accuracy is often misleading in such scenarios. A model that predicts the majority class for all instances can still achieve high accuracy, despite failing to identify minority class samples. Therefore, alternative metrics provide a more meaningful evaluation. Precision-recall (PR) curves are particularly useful in imbalanced classification, as they focus on the model's ability to correctly identify positive instances. Precision measures the proportion of correctly predicted positive instances out of all predicted positives, while recall quantifies the proportion of actual positive instances that were correctly identified. The F1-score, which is the harmonic mean of precision and recall, offers a balanced measure that accounts for both false positives and false negatives.

The receiver operating characteristic area under the curve (ROC-AUC) is another important metric that evaluates the model's ability to distinguish between classes across different classification thresholds. A model with a higher AUC value indicates a better trade-off between sensitivity and specificity. Balanced accuracy, which is the average recall for both classes, ensures that both the majority and minority classes are fairly represented in the evaluation process. These metrics provide a more comprehensive understanding of how well a model performs on imbalanced datasets, allowing practitioners to make informed decisions when selecting and tuning classification models.

Addressing class imbalance requires careful consideration of various techniques, including resampling strategies, cost-sensitive learning, ensemble methods, and hybrid approaches. Selecting the appropriate method depends on the specific characteristics of the dataset and the application domain. Additionally, using appropriate evaluation metrics ensures that model performance is accurately assessed, enabling the development of robust classifiers that effectively detect minority class instances.

Understanding Noisy Data

Noisy data is a common challenge in data analysis and machine learning, referring to errors, inconsistencies, or missing information within datasets. This noise can arise from various sources, including human errors during data entry, sensor malfunctions that produce inaccurate readings, and corruption of data due to transmission or storage issues. Regardless of the cause, noise can significantly impact the quality and reliability of data, ultimately affecting the performance of machine learning models.

One of the primary ways noises affects machine learning is by misleading the learning process, causing models to learn incorrect patterns. When a dataset contains mislabeled instances, models trained on this data may generalize poorly to new inputs, as they fail to distinguish between genuine patterns and random errors. This issue is particularly problematic in supervised learning, where labels guide the training process. If a significant portion of the data is mislabeled, the model might incorrectly associate input features with the wrong class, leading to erroneous predictions. For example, in medical diagnosis, if patient records contain misclassified disease labels, a machine learning model may learn unreliable associations between symptoms and conditions, ultimately affecting patient outcomes.

Another issue caused by noisy data is the introduction of inconsistencies, where duplicate records, conflicting values, or irregular formats exist within the dataset. These inconsistencies can arise from combining data from multiple sources, where different conventions or standards are used. If not addressed, inconsistencies can create confusion in pattern recognition, leading to unstable model predictions. For instance, in customer data analysis, if a single individual appears multiple times with slightly different names or addresses, the model may fail to recognize purchasing behavior patterns accurately.

Missing data is another form of noise that can disrupt machine learning models. Gaps in datasets occur due to various reasons, such as incomplete surveys, sensor failures, or issues in data collection processes. Missing values pose a challenge because many machine learning algorithms require complete data for training. Handling missing values improperly can result in biased models or loss of valuable information. Different strategies are used to address this issue, including imputation techniques that fill in missing values using statistical methods, deletion of incomplete records, or the use of algorithms that can handle missing data directly.

The presence of noise in data reduces the robustness of machine learning models, making them more sensitive to small variations in input data. When a model learns from a dataset containing a significant amount of noise, it may be overfit by memorizing noise rather than capturing the underlying structure of the data. Overfitting occurs when a model becomes too complex and performs exceptionally well on training data but fails to generalize to unseen examples. This problem is especially relevant in high-dimensional datasets, where spurious correlations caused by noise can lead to overly complex models with poor real-world performance.

To mitigate the effects of noise, data preprocessing techniques are commonly employed before training machine learning models. One approach is data cleaning, which involves detecting and correcting errors, removing duplicates, and standardizing data formats. For mislabeled data, algorithms such as noise filtering methods can be used to identify and correct potential misclassifications. Outlier detection techniques, including statistical methods and machine learning-based anomaly detection, help identify data points that deviate significantly from the expected distribution. Removing or adjusting these outliers can improve model accuracy and stability.

Feature engineering also plays a crucial role in handling noisy data by transforming raw data into a more useful format for machine learning models. Techniques such as feature selection and dimensionality reduction help eliminate irrelevant or noisy features, ensuring that models focus only on the most informative aspects of the data. Additionally, using robust machine learning algorithms that are less sensitive to noise, such as ensemble methods like Random Forests or boosting techniques, can enhance model performance in noisy environments. Noisy data presents a significant challenge in machine learning by introducing errors, inconsistencies, and missing information that can mislead models and reduce their robustness. The sources of noise are diverse, ranging from human errors to technical malfunctions, and their impact can be severe, leading to inaccurate predictions and poor generalization. Addressing noisy data requires careful preprocessing, including data cleaning, outlier detection, and robust feature engineering. By applying these techniques, machine learning models can become more resilient, ensuring they extract meaningful patterns from data while minimizing the influence of noise.

Techniques for Handling Noisy Data

Data cleaning and preprocessing are foundational steps in ensuring that machine learning models perform optimally, especially in the presence of noisy or incomplete data. The quality of data has a direct impact on model accuracy and generalizability, making it essential to apply rigorous preprocessing techniques before training a model. One of the most common challenges in preprocessing is handling missing values, which can occur due to various reasons, such as errors in data collection, sensor malfunctions, incomplete surveys, or system failures. If missing data is ignored or handled poorly, it can introduce biases and distort the learning process. There are several strategies for handling missing data, including imputation and deletion. Imputation methods fill in missing values based on statistical calculations such as mean, median, or mode imputation, where missing values are replaced with the most representative value from the available data. More sophisticated imputation techniques involve regression models, k-nearest neighbors (KNN), or deep learning-based approaches that predict missing values based on patterns found in other features of the dataset. However, when a significant proportion of a dataset contains missing values, imputation may not be reliable, and deletion of incomplete records might be necessary. While deletion can prevent unreliable patterns from influencing the model, it also reduces the dataset size and can lead to loss of potentially valuable information. A balance must be struck between preserving data quality and maintaining sufficient data for meaningful analysis.

Another critical aspect of data cleaning is detecting and removing outliers, which are data points that deviate significantly from the expected distribution. Outliers can occur due to measurement errors, incorrect data entry, or genuine rare events, and they can have a disproportionately large influence on machine learning models. The impact of outliers varies depending on the algorithm used; for example, linear regression models are highly sensitive to outliers, while tree-based models such as decision trees and random forests are more robust. Various methods exist for identifying outliers, including statistical approaches and machine learning-based anomaly detection techniques. The Z-score method, based on standard deviation, identifies data points that fall several standard deviations away from the mean, while the interquartile range (IQR) method considers values that fall outside a defined range as potential outliers. More advanced outlier detection methods include machine learning approaches like isolation forests, which detect anomalies by measuring how easily a data point can be isolated in a tree structure, and local outlier factor (LOF), which examines the density of neighboring points to determine whether a data point significantly deviates from the norm. Once outliers are identified, decisions must be made about how to handle them. In some cases, removing outliers is necessary, while in others, transforming the data using logarithmic scaling or winsorization (capping extreme values) can help mitigate their impact without discarding valuable information.

Label noise, which occurs when the labels assigned to training data are incorrect or inconsistent, is another major source of error in machine learning models. This can be caused by human errors during annotation, ambiguous labeling criteria, or unreliable data sources. If a model is trained on noisy labels, it may learn incorrect associations between features and output classes, leading to poor generalization. One approach to correcting label noise is bootstrapping, a technique where multiple models are trained on different subsets of the data to identify inconsistencies and refine the labels. Active learning methods, which involve selectively querying human annotators to review uncertain or suspicious labels, are also effective in improving label quality. In cases where label noise is suspected but difficult to correct manually, semi-supervised learning approaches can be employed, where a small portion of high confidence labeled data is used to guide the model in making predictions on noisy labels.

Choosing robust machine learning models can help mitigate the impact of noise in the data. Some algorithms are inherently more resistant to noise than others. Decision trees, random forests, and gradient boosting methods like XGBoost tend to be more robust to noisy data due to their ability to partition the feature space hierarchically and reduce the influence of individual noisy data points. Deep learning models can also be made more resilient through regularization techniques such as L1 and L2 regularization. L1 regularization, also known as Lasso, encourages sparsity in feature selection by penalizing large weights, while L2 regularization, known as Ridge regression, prevents the model from relying too heavily on any single feature by discouraging large weight values. Dropout, another regularization technique commonly used in neural networks, randomly disables a subset of neurons during training, forcing the model to learn more generalized patterns rather than memorizing specific noisy instances.

Data augmentation is a widely used technique to improve the robustness of machine learning models, especially in computer vision and natural language processing tasks. Augmentation involves artificially expanding the dataset by applying transformations such as noise injection, rotation, scaling, flipping, and translation to existing samples. This process helps models generalize better by exposing them to a wider variety of training examples, making them less sensitive to minor variations or noise in the input data. In image classification tasks, augmentation can significantly improve performance by ensuring that the model learns the fundamental features of objects rather than memorizing specific visual characteristics. In text-based datasets, augmentation techniques such as synonym replacement, back-translation (translating text to another language and back), and random word insertion can help improve model generalization while mitigating the impact of noisy text data.

Anomaly detection plays an essential role in identifying and handling noisy data. Various anomaly detection algorithms, such as autoencoders, one-class support vector machines (SVMs), and statistical methods, are used to flag potentially incorrect instances in datasets. Autoencoders, a type of neural network designed to learn efficient representations of data, can be trained on normal data to identify anomalies by measuring reconstruction errors—instances that deviate significantly from the expected pattern flagged as potential outliers. One-class SVMs attempt to find a decision boundary that encloses the majority of the normal data while isolating outliers. Statistical methods, such as Gaussian mixture models and Mahalanobis distance-based approaches, analyze the distribution of data points and detect those that fall far outside expected regions.

Best practices for training robust machine learning models begin with collecting high-quality data at the source. Ensuring accuracy at the data collection stage minimizes the need for extensive cleaning and prevents potential biases from affecting model performance. Cross-validation is a crucial technique for assessing model reliability, with stratified k-fold cross-validation ensuring that both majority and minority classes are well-represented in each fold of the training and validation sets. Proper monitoring of model performance is essential, and using evaluation metrics such as precision, recall, F1-score, and ROC-AUC helps in identifying potential overfitting to noisy data. Visualization tools such as confusion matrices, learning curves, and feature importance plots can provide insights into how the model is interpreting data and where potential issues might arise.

An iterative approach to improving data and models is key to maintaining robustness over time. Continuous feedback loops, where data is regularly reviewed and refined, ensure that errors and inconsistencies are gradually corrected. Human-in-the-loop approaches, where domain experts assist in refining model predictions and reviewing uncertain cases, can further improve performance, particularly in high-stakes applications such as healthcare and finance. Adversarial training, a technique where small perturbations are introduced into the input data to test the model's resilience, is another effective method for improving robustness. By training models to recognize and adapt to potential adversarial noise, they become better equipped to handle real-world data imperfections.

By implementing these strategies, machine learning practitioners can develop models that are more resilient to noisy data, ensuring higher accuracy, better generalization, and improved reliability across various applications.

In addition, handling imbalanced and noisy data is one of the most critical challenges in machine learning, as it directly affects model performance and generalization. When data is imbalanced, meaning that some classes are significantly underrepresented compared to others, machine learning models tend to develop a bias toward the majority class. This often results in poor detection of the minority class, which can be problematic in applications such as fraud detection, rare disease diagnosis, and spam filtering. Similarly, noisy data, which includes errors, inconsistencies, and missing values, can introduce inaccuracies and prevent models from learning meaningful patterns. Addressing these challenges requires a combination of resampling techniques, cost-sensitive learning, robust model selection, and effective data preprocessing strategies.

Resampling techniques are among the most widely used methods to handle imbalanced datasets. Oversampling methods such as the Synthetic Minority Oversampling Technique (SMOTE) generate synthetic examples of the minority class to balance the dataset. Instead of simply duplicating existing instances, SMOTE creates new samples by interpolating between existing minority class data points, making the dataset more representative. While oversampling increases the presence of the minority class, it can also lead to overfitting if not used carefully, as synthetic data may not always introduce meaningful variability. Undersampling, on the other hand, reduces the size of the majority class by randomly removing some of its instances, ensuring that both classes are more balanced. However, this technique runs the risk of discarding potentially valuable information. Hybrid approaches combine both oversampling and undersampling to maintain a balanced and informative dataset while reducing redundancy and overfitting risks.

Cost-sensitive learning is another approach that addresses class imbalances by assigning higher misclassification penalties to the minority class. Traditional machine learning models typically assume that all misclassifications carry equal cost, but in real-world scenarios, certain errors are more critical than others. In fraud detection, for example, failing to detect fraudulent transactions is far more damaging than mistakenly flagging legitimate transactions. By adjusting class weights or incorporating cost-sensitive loss functions, models can be trained to focus more on correctly identifying the minority class, even if the overall dataset remains imbalanced. Algorithms such as weighted decision trees, cost-sensitive support vector machines (SVMs), and deep learning models with modified loss functions allow practitioners to build classifiers that prioritize rare events without compromising overall accuracy.

Selecting robust machine learning models is crucial for handling both imbalanced and noisy data. Some algorithms are inherently more resistant to these challenges. Tree-based models such as random forests and gradient boosting algorithms like XGBoost can handle imbalanced data by learning from the structure of the dataset rather than relying purely on class frequencies. These models can assign different levels of importance to features and adjust decision boundaries dynamically, making them effective in identifying minority class instances. Deep learning architectures can also be adapted for imbalanced data by using class-weighted loss functions, data augmentation, or specialized sampling techniques. Regularization methods such as L1 and L2 regularization help mitigate the effects of noise by preventing models from overfitting outliers or errors in the training data.

Effective data preprocessing is essential for reducing the impact of noise. Noisy data can come from a variety of sources, including human error, sensor malfunctions, or incomplete information. Handling missing values is a key part of preprocessing, as gaps in data can distort learning patterns and lead to biased models. Common techniques for dealing with missing values include mean or median imputation, where missing values are replaced with a representative statistic, and model-based imputation, where missing values are predicted using other features. In some cases, particularly when data is missing at random, dropping incomplete records is a viable option, though it should be done with caution to avoid unnecessary data loss.

Outliers, which are extreme values that deviate significantly from the expected distribution, can also introduce noise into machine learning models. Detecting and handling outliers involves statistical techniques such as the Z-score method, which measures how many standard deviations a data point is from the mean, or the interquartile range (IQR) method, which identifies values falling outside a normal range. More advanced approaches, such as isolation forests and local outlier factor (LOF), leverage machine learning to identify anomalous points in large and high-dimensional datasets. Once outliers are identified, practitioners must decide whether to remove, transform, or retain them based on their impact on model performance.

Label noise, where data labels are incorrect or inconsistent, poses another significant challenge in supervised learning. Mislabeled data can arise due to human annotation errors, ambiguous classification criteria, or unreliable data sources. If not addressed, label noise can lead to incorrect model training, reducing overall accuracy and generalization ability. Techniques such as bootstrapping, which involves sampling multiple subsets of data to verify label consistency, and active learning, where human annotators are asked to review uncertain labels, can help refine datasets. In deep learning, semi-supervised approaches allow models to leverage a small set of high-confidence labels while learning from noisy data.

Beyond preprocessing, anomaly detection plays a critical role in managing noisy data. Anomaly detection algorithms, such as autoencoders and one-class SVMs, help identify potentially incorrect instances in datasets. Autoencoders, which are neural networks trained to reconstruct normal data patterns, can flag anomalies by measuring reconstruction errors—instances that deviate significantly from expected patterns are considered noisy or erroneous. One-class SVMs create decision boundaries that enclose normal data while isolating outliers, making them effective for detecting noise in high-dimensional datasets.

Ensuring the reliability of machine learning models also requires continuous monitoring and iterative improvements. Simply training a model once and deploying without ongoing evaluation can lead to performance degradation over time, particularly in dynamic environments where data distributions change. Implementing cross-validation techniques, such as stratified k-fold cross-validation, ensures that models are tested on multiple subsets of data to improve generalization. Regular model evaluation using precision-recall curves, F1-score, and ROC-AUC helps detect issues with class imbalance and noisy data that may not be visible through traditional accuracy metrics. Visualization tools such as confusion matrices and t-SNE plots provide insights into how the model is classifying different data points and where potential misclassifications occur.

Model optimization is an ongoing process that requires adapting to changes in data distribution and real-world variability. Collecting high-quality data at the source is the first step toward ensuring robust model performance, but as new data becomes available, it is essential to update models and retrain them to reflect current patterns. Human-in-the-loop strategies, where domain experts review model predictions and provide corrections, enhance model reliability, particularly in high-stakes applications such as healthcare and finance. Adversarial training, a technique where small perturbations are introduced into input data to test the model's resilience, can further improve robustness by ensuring that the model learns meaningful patterns rather than memorizing noise.

Deploying reliable AI solutions in real-world applications requires models that perform well despite data imperfections. The key to success lies in combining multiple strategies, from resampling techniques and cost-sensitive learning to robust preprocessing and continuous monitoring. As data landscapes evolve, machine learning practitioners must remain proactive in refining data quality, improving model architectures, and optimizing evaluation metrics.

6

The Art of Hyperparameter Tuning

Hyperparameter tuning is a critical step in machine learning model development, as it directly influences a model's ability to generalize well to unseen data. Unlike parameters, which are learned from the data during training, hyperparameters must be set before training begins and control various aspects of the learning process. Some of the most common hyperparameters include the learning rate in gradient-based optimization, the number of layers and neurons in a neural network, the regularization strength in linear models, and the number of trees in ensemble methods like random forests. Selecting the right hyperparameters can significantly improve model performance, while poor choices can lead to issues such as overfitting, underfitting, slow convergence, or excessive computational costs. Overfitting occurs when a model becomes too complex and memorizes the training data rather than learning general patterns, leading to poor performance on new data. Underfitting, on the other hand, happens when a model is too simple to capture the underlying structure of the data, resulting in high bias and low accuracy. Hyperparameter tuning is, therefore, a delicate balance between optimizing performance and ensuring that the model remains generalizable. Since hyperparameter spaces are often high-dimensional and nonlinear, finding the optimal combination requires systematic experimentation rather than arbitrary selection. The process is particularly crucial in deep learning, where models have many tunable components, and training times can be long. Without proper hyperparameter tuning, even the most advanced algorithms may fail to perform effectively, highlighting the importance of a structured approach to optimizing model settings.

Understanding Hyperparameters

Hyperparameters play a fundamental role in shaping how a machine learning model learns from data, affecting not only its accuracy but also its efficiency and generalization ability. Unlike parameters, which are derived from the training process, hyperparameters must be defined before training begins and require careful tuning to strike the right balance between underfitting and overfitting. Choosing the appropriate hyperparameter values can significantly improve model performance, while poor choices may lead to suboptimal results, excessive computational costs, or an inability to generalize to new data.

One of the most important hyperparameters in machine learning, particularly in deep learning, is the learning rate. The learning rate dictates how much the model updates its weights with each iteration of training. A learning rate that is too high can cause the optimization process to overshoot the optimal solution, preventing convergence and leading to erratic model behavior. In contrast, a learning rate that is too low can result in sluggish training, where the model takes too long to learn or gets stuck in local minima, failing to reach the global optimal point. To address these challenges, learning rate scheduling techniques, such as step decay, exponential decay, and adaptive learning rate algorithms like Adam and RMSprop, are used to dynamically adjust the learning rate during training. These techniques help stabilize training and accelerate convergence without overshooting.

Batch size is another key hyperparameter, particularly in neural networks and deep learning models. It determines the number of training samples processed before the model's weights are updated. Small batch sizes provide more frequent updates, introducing randomness that can help the model escape local minima and improve generalization. However, smaller batches also introduce more variance in the gradient updates, which may lead to instability in training. On the other hand, larger batch sizes result in smoother updates and reduced training variance but require more memory and computational resources. They may also lead to poor generalization if the model becomes too reliant on the patterns observed in each batch rather than learning a more general representation of the data. Finding the right batch size often requires experimentation, balancing computational efficiency with model performance.

In deep learning architectures, the number of layers and neurons per layer plays a critical role in determining the network's complexity and capacity. A shallow network with too few neurons may lack the ability to capture intricate patterns within the data, leading to underfitting. Conversely, an excessively deep network with too many neurons can lead to overfitting, where the model memorizes the training data instead of learning generalizable features. The depth of the network and the number of neurons in each layer must be carefully selected based on the complexity of the task. Techniques such as dropout, batch normalization, and residual connections are often used to mitigate the risks associated with deep networks, ensuring that the model remains both powerful and generalizable.

Regularization techniques help prevent overfitting by controlling the complexity of a model. L1 regularization, also known as Lasso regression, encourages sparsity by pushing some weights to zero, effectively performing feature selection. This technique is useful when working with high-dimensional datasets where many features may be irrelevant. L2 regularization, or Ridge regression, penalizes large weight values, encouraging the model to distribute importance across multiple features rather than relying too heavily on a few. Dropout is a widely used regularization technique in neural networks, where random neurons are disabled during training to prevent co-adaptation among neurons. By forcing the model to learn redundant representations, dropout improves generalization and robustness.

For decision-making tree-based models, tree depth is a critical hyperparameter that dictates how flexible or restrictive the model is. A shallow decision tree may struggle to capture complex relationships in the data, leading to underfitting. However, an overly deep tree can memorize training examples, making it highly sensitive to noise and leading to overfitting. To strike a balance, techniques such as pruning, setting a maximum depth, or defining the minimum number of samples required to split a node can be used to limit tree complexity while maintaining predictive power. In ensemble methods like random forests and gradient boosting, additional hyperparameters such as the number of trees, learning rate, and minimum sample splits further influence model performance.

Support vector machines (SVMs) rely on kernel functions to transform data into higher-dimensional spaces, allowing the model to find optimal decision boundaries even in non-linearly separable cases. The choice of kernel function is a crucial hyperparameter that affects how well the SVM can classify data. A linear kernel works well for datasets where the classes can be separated by a straight line, while polynomial and radial basis function (RBF) kernels allow for more flexible decision boundaries that can capture complex relationships. Tuning kernel parameters, such as the degree of the polynomial kernel or the gamma parameter in the RBF kernel, is essential for optimizing the SVM's performance.

Hyperparameter tuning is an iterative and often computationally expensive process, but it is essential for achieving optimal model performance. Several methods exist for searching the best hyperparameter combinations. Grid search systematically evaluates all possible combinations of hyperparameters within a predefined range, but it can be inefficient when dealing with high-dimensional search spaces. Random search, on the other hand, samples hyperparameter values randomly within a given range, which can be more efficient in some cases. More advanced approaches, such as Bayesian optimization, use probabilistic models to intelligently explore the hyperparameter space, focusing on promising regions and reducing the number of evaluations needed to find an optimal configuration.

The impact of hyperparameter tuning extends beyond individual model performance. Well-tuned hyperparameters can significantly reduce training time, improve generalization to new data, and make models more robust in real-world applications. A carefully optimized model not only achieves higher accuracy but also ensures that computational resources are used efficiently. Given the complexity of modern machine learning models, automated hyperparameter tuning techniques and tools, such as Optuna, Hyperopt, and AutoML frameworks, are increasingly being adopted to streamline the optimization process.

Ultimately, hyperparameters serve as the fine-tuning controls that dictate how a machine learning model learns, adapts, and performs on a given dataset. Their selection requires both theoretical understanding and empirical experimentation. By leveraging structured tuning approaches and continuous monitoring, machine learning practitioners can ensure that their models achieve the best possible balance between accuracy, efficiency, and generalization.

Systematic Approaches to Hyperparameter Optimization

There are several strategies for tuning hyperparameters, ranging from simple manual adjustments to sophisticated automated methods that use machine learning to refine the tuning process. One of the most basic approaches is manual tuning, where a practitioner adjusts hyperparameters based on intuition, experience, or trial and error. While this method can sometimes be effective, it is highly inefficient and impractical for complex models with many hyperparameters. A more structured approach is grid search, where a predefined set of hyperparameter values is systematically tested, and the combination yielding the best performance is selected. Grid search is exhaustive, meaning it evaluates all possible combinations within the specified range, but it quickly becomes computationally expensive as the number of hyperparameters increases. For example, if a model has three hyperparameters and each can take ten values, grid search would require testing 1,000 different configurations, making it inefficient for large search spaces.

An alternative to grid search is random search, where hyperparameter values are sampled randomly within specified ranges rather than testing all possible combinations. This approach is often more efficient than grid search because it explores a wider variety of hyperparameter values without testing unnecessary configurations. Research has shown that random search often finds near optimal hyperparameter settings in a fraction of the time required for grid search, especially when only a few hyperparameters have a significant impact on performance. More advanced techniques, such as Bayesian optimization, take a probabilistic approach to hyperparameter tuning by iteratively selecting the most promising values based on past evaluations. Unlike grid and random search, Bayesian optimization builds a model of the relationship between hyperparameters and performance, then uses this model to make informed choices about which hyperparameter combinations to evaluate next. This allows it to focus on the most promising areas of the search space, reducing the number of required evaluations and improving efficiency. Bayesian optimization is particularly useful for deep learning models, where hyperparameter tuning can be computationally expensive and time-consuming.

Other methods include evolutionary algorithms and reinforcement learning-based tuning, which use iterative processes to refine hyperparameters based on performance feedback. Evolutionary algorithms simulate the process of natural selection, generating populations of hyperparameter configurations and evolving them over multiple iterations by selecting the best-performing ones and introducing variations through mutation and crossover. Reinforcement learning-based tuning, on the other hand, treats hyperparameter selection as a sequential decision-making problem and uses reinforcement learning agents to explore different configurations.

These advanced techniques are particularly beneficial when tuning deep neural networks, which have large, complex search spaces and require more sophisticated optimization strategies. Another increasingly popular approach is Hyperband, which dynamically allocates computational resources to different hyperparameter configurations based on their early performance, allowing poorly performing configurations to be discarded quickly and focusing resources on the most promising ones.

Best Practices for Efficient and Reliable Hyperparameter Tuning

To achieve effective hyperparameter tuning, it is essential to establish clear evaluation criteria and avoid biases that may lead to misleading conclusions. The choice of performance metric plays a crucial role in assessing model quality, especially in applications with class imbalance or complex decision boundaries. For instance, traditional accuracy is not always an appropriate metric, particularly in imbalanced datasets where precision-recall curves, F1-score, and area under the ROC curve (AUC-ROC) provide better insights into model performance. Cross-validation techniques, such as k-fold cross-validation, help ensure that hyperparameter tuning results are robust and not overly dependent on a specific training-test split. Instead of relying on a single train-test partition, cross-validation repeatedly splits the dataset into multiple subsets, training and evaluating the model on different combinations of the data. This reduces the risk of overfitting and ensures that the selected hyperparameters generalize well to unseen data.

Overfitting can be a major issue in hyperparameter tuning, as models may perform exceptionally well on the validation set but fail to generalize to new data. Regularization techniques, such as L1 and L2 penalties in regression models or dropout in deep learning, help prevent overfitting by discouraging excessively complex models. Early stopping is another important technique in deep learning, where training is halted when performance on a validation set starts to degrade, preventing the model from overfitting to training noise. Learning curves and diagnostic plots can provide valuable insights into whether a model is underfitting or overfitting, guiding hyperparameter adjustments accordingly.

Automating the hyperparameter tuning process can significantly improve efficiency and reduce human effort. Several libraries, such as Optuna, Hyperopt, and Google's Vizier, provide automated hyperparameter tuning frameworks that use advanced optimization techniques to find the best hyperparameter configurations with minimal manual intervention. In deep learning, libraries like Keras Tuner and Ray Tune streamline hyperparameter searches by integrating seamlessly with existing model architectures. When tuning deep learning models, learning rate scheduling can improve convergence by gradually reducing the learning rate over time, preventing the model from overshooting optimal solutions. Other techniques, such as batch normalization and adaptive optimizers like Adam and RMSprop, help stabilize training and reduce sensitivity to initial hyperparameter settings.

The key to effective hyperparameter tuning is to strike a balance between model complexity, computational efficiency, and generalization. A well-tuned model not only achieves high accuracy but also maintains robustness across different datasets and real-world scenarios. By combining systematic search strategies, cross-validation, and regularization techniques, machine learning practitioners can optimize hyperparameters efficiently while avoiding common pitfalls. As models and datasets grow in complexity, leveraging automated hyperparameter tuning frameworks and advanced optimization techniques will become increasingly essential for building reliable AI systems. Hyperparameter tuning is not a one-time process but an ongoing optimization challenge that requires continuous experimentation and refinement to ensure that machine learning models perform at their best in dynamic environments.

Hyperparameter tuning is an essential process in machine learning that determines how well a model learns from data. Unlike model parameters, which are learned during training, hyperparameters must be set before training begins and play a crucial role in controlling model behavior. Effective hyperparameter tuning ensures that a model achieves the best possible balance between accuracy, generalization, and computational efficiency. Choosing the right tuning approach depends on several factors, including available computational resources, dataset size, and model complexity.

One of the simplest methods for hyperparameter tuning is Grid Search, which systematically explores all possible combinations of predefined hyperparameter values. This method guarantees that the best combination within the search space is found, but it comes at a high computational cost. Grid Search is most effective when dealing with relatively small hyperparameter spaces, as evaluating every combination becomes impractical as the number of parameters and possible values increases. In high-dimensional search spaces, the computational burden can quickly become overwhelming, making Grid Search an inefficient choice for complex models.

Random Search offers an alternative that reduces computational costs while still providing effective tuning. Instead of exhaustively evaluating every combination, Random Search selects hyperparameter values at random from a specified range. This approach allows for broader exploration of the hyperparameter space without the rigidity of Grid Search. While it does not guarantee finding the absolute best combination, studies have shown that Random Search often yields similar or even better results than Grid Search in a fraction of the time, particularly when certain hyperparameters have a greater impact on model performance than others.

For more advanced optimization, Bayesian Optimization provides a smarter, more efficient way to tune hyperparameters by using probabilistic models to guide the search. Instead of selecting hyperparameters randomly or systematically, Bayesian Optimization builds a surrogate model, usually a Gaussian Process, to predict which hyperparameter settings are likely to yield the best performance. It then updates this model based on observed results, focusing the search on promising regions of the hyperparameter space. This approach significantly reduces the number of evaluations needed to find an optimal solution, making it well-suited for complex models that require expensive computations. Bayesian Optimization is particularly useful when training deep learning models or other algorithms that take a long time to evaluate, as it optimizes the tuning process without requiring exhaustive testing.

Another powerful hyperparameter tuning technique is the use of Genetic Algorithms, which take inspiration from natural selection to evolve hyperparameter configurations over multiple generations. In this approach, an initial population of hyperparameter sets is generated, and their performance is evaluated based on a chosen metric. The best-performing configurations are then selected and combined to create a new generation, incorporating elements of crossover and mutation to introduce variation. Over successive generations, the algorithm converges toward an optimal set of hyperparameters. Genetic Algorithms are especially effective when dealing with large, complex search spaces where traditional methods struggle. They allow for exploration beyond predefined search grids and have been successfully applied to deep learning and neural architecture search.

In addition to these tuning techniques, practical considerations must be taken into account to ensure efficient and effective hyperparameter optimization. The choice of tuning method depends on the available computational resources and time constraints. For small models with limited hyperparameter spaces, Grid Search may be sufficient, while Random Search offers a good balance of efficiency and effectiveness for moderately complex models. Bayesian Optimization and Genetic Algorithms are best suited for deep learning and other computationally intensive applications where tuning costs are high, as they intelligently explore the search space and require fewer iterations to find optimal configurations.

Beyond selecting the right tuning method, best practices in hyperparameter tuning include using cross-validation to ensure robustness, monitoring model performance metrics over multiple iterations, and leveraging distributed computing or cloud-based optimization frameworks when handling large-scale problems. Automated machine learning (AutoML) platforms also integrate these tuning strategies to streamline the process, making it easier for practitioners to optimize their models without extensive manual intervention.

Ultimately, hyperparameter tuning is a critical component of building high-performance machine learning models. The ability to find the right balance between accuracy, efficiency, and generalization is key to ensuring that models perform well in real-world applications. By combining systematic tuning strategies with the best practices, machine learning practitioners can significantly enhance model performance, leading to more reliable predictions and better decision-making across various domains.

7

Interpretability and Explainability in Machine Learning

As machine learning models become more complex and widely adopted, the need for interpretability and explainability has become critical. Stakeholders—including data scientists, business executives, regulators, and end users—need to understand how models make decisions to ensure fairness, trust, and compliance with ethical standards. Interpretability refers to the ability to understand how a model arrives at its predictions, while explainability extends this by providing reasons for those predictions in a way that is meaningful to different stakeholders. In high-stakes applications such as healthcare, finance, and criminal justice, explainability is essential for decision-making, risk management, and regulatory compliance. Without clear explanations, even highly accurate models can be met with skepticism and resistance, limiting their adoption and effectiveness.

Building Trust in AI Systems

Trust is a fundamental requirement for the widespread adoption of machine learning models, particularly in fields where decisions have significant consequences for individuals and society. Interpretability in AI ensures that users can understand how and why a model arrives at specific predictions, fostering confidence in its outputs. When stakeholders can verify that a model's reasoning aligns with domain expertise and common sense, they are more likely to trust and integrate AI-driven decisions into their workflows.

Industries such as healthcare, finance, and criminal justice heavily rely on trust in AI systems. For example, in medical diagnostics, a doctor must have confidence in an AI system's recommendation before acting on it. If the model's decision-making process is opaque, medical professionals may hesitate to use it, potentially missing out on the benefits AI can provide.

Ensuring Fairness and Mitigating Bias

Machine learning models are trained in historical data, which may contain biases reflecting societal inequalities. If left unchecked, these biases can lead to unfair and discriminatory outcomes, disproportionately affecting certain groups based on gender, race, or socioeconomic status. Interpretability allows practitioners to examine how a model makes its decisions and whether it exhibits biased behavior.

Several techniques can be employed to promote fairness in AI models. Fairness audits, for example, systematically evaluate whether a model's predictions disadvantage particular demographics. Counterfactual analysis, another powerful method, involves assessing whether a model's decision would change if certain attributes of an individual were altered while keeping everything else constant. By incorporating these interpretability tools, organizations can detect and mitigate bias, ensuring that AI systems are fair and do not reinforce existing disparities.

Regulatory Compliance and Legal Accountability

Regulatory frameworks around the world increasingly demand transparency in automated decision-making. For instance, the European Union's General Data Protection Regulation (GDPR) grants individuals the right to receive explanations for automated decisions that significantly impact them. Similarly, financial institutions in various countries must adhere to regulations that require explainability in credit scoring and loan approval processes.

Failure to comply with these regulations can result in legal consequences, financial penalties, and reputational damage. By ensuring interpretability, organizations can provide clear, comprehensible justifications for their models' decisions, making it easier to defend them in legal settings. Moreover, regulatory bodies can audit AI models more effectively when their decision-making processes are transparent, reinforcing accountability and ethical AI deployment.

Improving Model Debugging and Performance

Model interpretability plays a crucial role in diagnosing errors, improving accuracy, and optimizing machine learning performance. Understanding why a model makes specific predictions helps data scientists identify weaknesses and refine models accordingly. If a model consistently misclassifies certain inputs, interpretability tools can highlight whether the issue stems from poor data quality, improper feature selection, or flawed algorithmic assumptions.

For instance, feature importance analysis can reveal which variables most influence a model's predictions. If irrelevant or misleading features have disproportionate influence, retraining the model with better feature engineering can enhance its reliability. Similarly, methods like SHAP (Shapley Additive Explanations) and LIME (Local Interpretable Model-Agnostic Explanations) help data scientists visualize how individual features contribute to specific decisions, enabling them to fine-tune models for better performance.

Enhancing Human-AI Collaboration

In many real-world applications, machine learning models function as decision-support tools rather than standalone decision-makers. In healthcare, AI-assisted diagnostics provide insights that help doctors make informed treatment decisions. In finance, credit risk models support loan officers in assessing applicants. In cybersecurity, AI-driven fraud detection systems flag suspicious transactions for further investigation by analysts.

For these human-AI collaborations to be effective, model interpretability is essential. When users can understand the reasoning behind an AI recommendation, they are better equipped to incorporate it into their decision-making processes. For example, a physician using an AI diagnostic tool needs to know why the model suggests a particular diagnosis. If the model highlights relevant medical features—such as lab results or imaging anomalies—the doctor can verify the AI's reasoning and make a more informed decision.

Furthermore, interpretable models enable practitioners to provide better explanations to end-users affected by AI-driven decisions. A rejected loan applicant, for example, may be given a clear, data-driven explanation for why their application was denied, along with actionable steps to improve their eligibility. This transparency not only improves the user experience but also reinforces trust in AI-driven decision-making.

As machine learning becomes increasingly integrated into critical aspects of society, ensuring interpretability is not just a technical necessity but an ethical imperative. Transparent models build trust, promote fairness, facilitate regulatory compliance, improve debugging and performance, and enhance human-AI collaboration. Organizations that prioritize interpretability in their AI systems stand to gain not only from increased adoption and regulatory alignment but also from more ethical and responsible AI deployment. In the pursuit of AI advancement, interpretability should remain a central guiding principle, ensuring that technology serves humanity in a transparent, fair, and accountable manner.

Approaches to Model Interpretability

Model interpretability is a critical aspect of machine learning, as it enables users to understand how models arrive at their predictions. This is particularly important in high-stakes applications such as healthcare, finance, and criminal justice, where transparency and trust in the model's decisions are essential. There are two primary approaches to model interpretability: using inherently interpretable models that offer transparency by design and applying post-hoc explanation techniques to analyze complex black-box models.

One of the most straightforward ways to ensure interpretability is to use models that are intrinsically transparent. Linear regression and logistic regression fall into this category because their mathematical structure allows for a direct understanding of how input variables influence the predicted outcome. In a linear regression model, each independent variable is assigned a coefficient that represents its weight or contribution to the prediction. If a coefficient is positive, it means that increasing the corresponding feature value will increase the predicted outcome, whereas a negative coefficient indicates an inverse relationship. Logistic regression follows a similar principle but is used for classification tasks, where it maps input features to probabilities through the logistic function. The coefficients in logistic regression help explain how much each feature contributes to pushing the probability of a particular class higher or lower. These models are widely used in scenarios where interpretability is required, such as credit scoring and medical diagnostics.

Decision trees provide another layer of interpretability by structuring decisions in a hierarchical manner. A decision tree consists of nodes that represent feature splits, with each branch leading to either another split or a final prediction. Since decision trees make decisions based on simple if-then conditions, they are easy to understand and trace. For example, a decision tree model predicting whether a customer will default on a loan might first check whether their income is above a certain threshold. If not, it might then look at their credit score to make a final decision. This sequential decision-making process makes it possible for users to follow the logic behind a prediction, making decision trees a preferred choice in domains where explainability is crucial.

Another type of intrinsically interpretable model is the rule-based model. These models extract human-readable rules from data, which makes them particularly useful in applications where decisions must be justified. RuleFit, for example, is an algorithm that combines linear models with decision rules to create interpretable rule-based predictions. These rules provide explicit conditions under which certain outcomes occur, making it easier for domain experts and stakeholders to validate model behavior.

When dealing with more complex models, such as deep neural networks or ensemble methods like random forests and gradient boosting machines, additional techniques are required to interpret their decisions. Feature importance analysis is one such approach, as it helps quantify the influence of individual features on predictions. Two of the most widely used feature importance methods are SHAP (Shapley Additive Explanations) and LIME (Local Interpretable Model-agnostic Explanations).

SHAP is based on cooperative game theory and assigns a contribution score to each feature for every individual prediction. It computes these scores by considering all possible combinations of features and evaluating their impact on the prediction. The result is a set of SHAP values that indicate how much each feature contributed to moving the prediction away from a baseline value. For example, in a medical diagnosis model, SHAP could reveal that a high cholesterol level contributed 30% to the probability of predicting heart disease, while a low blood pressure value reduced that probability by 15%. This level of detail allows practitioners to understand not just which features are important but also how they interact to influence the final decision.

LIME, on the other hand, takes a different approach by creating a locally interpretable approximation of the model. Instead of trying to explain the entire model at once, LIME focuses on explaining individual predictions by generating small perturbations in the input data and observing how the model's output changes. It then fits a simple, interpretable model—such as a linear model—around the perturbed samples to approximate the decision boundary of the complex model. This allows users to understand why a specific input led to a particular prediction, even when dealing with highly nonlinear models.

Another technique for improving interpretability in complex models is the use of partial dependence plots (PDPs) and individual conditional expectation (ICE) plots. PDPs show the average effect of a single feature on the model's predictions while keeping all other features constant. This provides a high-level view of how a feature influences the outcome. For instance, a PDP for a house price prediction model might show that increasing the number of bedrooms leads to higher prices, but the effect plateaus beyond a certain point. While PDPs provide useful insights, they only show average trends and may obscure variations in individual instances. ICE plots address this limitation by displaying the effect of a feature at the level of individual data points. Instead of aggregating results, ICE plots show how a particular prediction changes as one feature varies while holding all others fixed. This makes ICE plots particularly useful for capturing interactions between variables that might not be apparent in a PDP.

Counterfactual explanations take a different approach to interpretability by answering "what-if" questions. Instead of explaining why a model made a particular prediction, counterfactual explanations focus on what changes would have led to a different outcome. For example, in a loan approval model, a counterfactual explanation might indicate: "If the applicant's annual income were $5,000 higher and their credit score was 50 points higher, the loan would have been approved." These explanations are particularly valuable in fields like finance and healthcare, where users need actionable insights to modify their inputs and achieve the desired outcome. Counterfactuals also provide a way to detect and address potential biases in machine learning models by identifying situations where small, seemingly insignificant changes in input values lead to drastically different predictions.

Deep learning models, particularly those based on transformers and attention mechanisms, pose additional challenges in interpretability due to their complexity. However, attention mechanisms offer a way to gain insights into how these models process information. Attention-based models highlight the most relevant parts of the input data, making it easier to understand their decision-making process. In natural language processing (NLP), for example, attention maps can show which words a model focused on when classifying a piece of text. In a sentiment analysis task, an attention-based model might assign higher weights to words like "excellent" or "terrible," revealing which parts of the input influenced its decision. Similarly, in machine translation, attention maps can indicate how a model aligns words from the source language to the target language, helping researchers diagnose errors and improve model performance.

Ultimately, model interpretability is essential for building trust in machine learning systems, ensuring fairness, and improving accountability. While simple, transparent models provide an intuitive understanding of decision-making processes, more complex models require post-hoc explanation techniques such as feature importance analysis, partial dependence plots, counterfactual explanations, and attention mechanisms. By leveraging these methods, practitioners can make machine learning models more understandable, leading to more informed decision-making and greater adoption of AI-driven solutions in real-world applications.

Challenges and Trade-offs in Explainability

Model explainability in machine learning presents several challenges and trade-offs that practitioners must navigate. One of the most significant trade-offs is accuracy and interpretability. Simple models such as linear regression, logistic regression, and decision trees are inherently interpretable, meaning their decision-making process is transparent and easy to understand. However, these models may lack the predictive power needed for complex real-world problems. In contrast, more sophisticated models, such as deep neural networks, gradient boosting machines, and ensemble methods, often achieve higher accuracy by capturing intricate patterns in data. The downside is that these models function as black boxes, making it difficult to understand how they arrive at their predictions.

This trade-off creates a dilemma for machine learning practitioners. In some applications, such as healthcare and finance, where interpretability is crucial for regulatory compliance and ethical considerations, it may be necessary to sacrifice some predictive power in favor of transparency. For example, in a credit scoring model, regulators and financial institutions require an explanation of why a particular loan application was approved or denied. In such cases, using an interpretable model, even at the cost of slightly lower accuracy, may be preferable to a highly accurate but opaque deep learning model. Conversely, in applications like image recognition or speech processing, where accuracy is the primary concern, black-box models may be acceptable despite their lack of interpretability.

To balance accuracy and interpretability, hybrid approaches have been developed. One such approach is the use of explainability tools that analyze complex models post-hoc, providing insights into their decision-making process. Techniques such as SHAP (Shapley Additive Explanations), LIME (Local Interpretable Model-agnostic Explanations), and counterfactual explanations allow practitioners to extract interpretable insights from black-box models without compromising their predictive power. Another approach is model distillation, where a complex model is trained first, and then a simpler, more interpretable model is trained to mimic its behavior. This enables users to approximate the decision boundaries of the original model while gaining some level of interpretability.

Scalability is another major challenge in model explainability, particularly as datasets and models grow in size. Many interpretability techniques, such as SHAP, become computationally expensive when applied to large-scale models with thousands or millions of features. As the complexity of a model increases, the number of possible feature interactions grows exponentially, making it difficult to provide meaningful explanations in a reasonable time frame. Additionally, in deep learning models with billions of parameters, techniques like attention visualization and feature attribution can become overwhelming, making it hard to extract useful insights.

To address scalability challenges, researchers have developed techniques such as hierarchical explanations, where interpretability methods focus on high-level patterns before zooming in on individual predictions. This allows for a structured approach to explanation, making it easier to analyze large models. Another solution is model distillation, where the original complex model is replaced with a smaller, interpretable approximation. For example, a deep neural network can be distilled into a decision tree or a linear model that retains much of the original model's predictive capability while being easier to interpret. These methods help ensure that explainability remains feasible even as machine learning models scale up in complexity.

A further challenge lies in the distinction between technical interpretability and human interpretability. A technically sound explanation, such as a set of SHAP values indicating feature importance, may not always be meaningful to end users. Different stakeholders have varying needs when it comes to model explanations.

Data scientists and machine learning engineers often require detailed insights into feature importance, feature interactions, and statistical relationships within the model. For them, granular explanations that provide mathematical justifications for model predictions are valuable. However, business executives and decision-makers typically do not have the technical expertise to interpret such detailed explanations. Instead, they require high-level insights that relate model decisions to business goals. For example, in an e-commerce setting, a marketing executive may not need to understand the inner workings of a recommendation algorithm but may need a clear summary of how customer behavior influences product recommendations.

End users, who are directly impacted by model decisions, require a different level of explanation. For them, an explanation should be intuitive, actionable, and relevant to their needs. If a model denies a loan application, the applicant needs to understand why and what they can do to improve their chances of approval in the future. Providing a counterfactual explanation such as "If your annual income were $5,000 higher, your loan would have been approved" is far more useful than a technical breakdown of feature importance scores. Ensuring that model explanations are understandable to non-technical users is critical for building trust and fostering adoption of machine learning systems.

The challenge of human interpretability is particularly pronounced in industries where AI-driven decisions affect individuals' lives, such as healthcare, hiring, and law enforcement. In these fields, a lack of clear explanations can lead to distrust, resistance to AI adoption, and potential ethical concerns. For instance, if a deep learning model is used to diagnose diseases but provides no explanation for its predictions, doctors may be reluctant to trust its recommendations. In such cases, explainability methods like attention visualization, concept activation, and counterfactual reasoning can help bridge the gap between technical and human interpretability.

Overall, model explainability involves navigating trade-offs between accuracy and transparency, addressing scalability challenges, and ensuring that explanations are meaningful to different stakeholders. While simple models offer interpretability at the cost of predictive power, complex models require post-hoc techniques to provide insights into their decision-making processes. As machine learning continues to evolve, improving interpretability methods will be essential for ensuring that AI-driven systems are transparent, accountable, and aligned with human values.

Best Practices for Making Models Transparent and Actionable

Ensuring that machine learning models are transparent and actionable requires adopting best practices that prioritize interpretability, fairness, and regulatory compliance. One of the most important aspects of making models interpretable is choosing the right level of explanation for the target audience. Different stakeholders require different types of explanations based on their level of technical expertise and their role in decision-making. For non-technical stakeholders such as business executives, policymakers, or end users, explanations should be presented in a way that is easy to understand. This can be achieved through visualizations, such as feature importance plots or heatmaps, as well as through natural language summaries that describe the model's decision-making process in simple terms. For example, in an AI-powered hiring system, a candidate receiving feedback about their application should be given an intuitive explanation like, "Your application was not shortlisted because your experience in data analysis was below the required threshold."

Providing such explanations helps build trust and ensures that users understand how decisions are made.

On the other hand, technical stakeholders such as data scientists, machine learning engineers, and regulatory bodies require more detailed explanations. These explanations should include mathematical justifications, statistical analyses, and documentation on how features influence model predictions. Techniques such as SHAP (Shapley Additive Explanations), LIME (Local Interpretable Model-agnostic Explanations), and partial dependence plots (PDPs) provide granular insights into how the model behaves. A data scientist analyzing a fraud detection model, for example, may need a detailed breakdown of how individual features contribute to the model's prediction of fraudulent transactions. Providing this level of technical transparency ensures that models can be audited, debugged, and improved effectively.

The crucial best practice for model transparency is leveraging model-agnostic explanation techniques. Since different machine learning models vary in complexity, using explanation methods that can be applied to any model ensures consistency and flexibility in interpretability efforts. Model-agnostic methods such as SHAP, LIME, and PDPs can be used across different algorithms, including neural networks, decision trees, and ensemble methods. This versatility makes them useful for organizations that work with multiple machine learning models across different applications. Model-agnostic techniques allow for uniformity in explainability approaches, ensuring that stakeholders receive comparable insights regardless of the model being used.

Another key practice in making models interpretable is testing for fairness and bias regularly. Machine learning models are susceptible to biases, either due to biased training data or structural issues within the model itself. Bias can lead to unfair or discriminatory outcomes, which is particularly concerning in sensitive applications such as hiring, lending, and criminal justice. To mitigate these risks, organizations should implement fairness metrics and bias detection tools to ensure that model decisions do not disproportionately affect certain groups. Fairness audits can be conducted by evaluating whether the model produces disparate outcomes across different demographic groups. For example, in a loan approval model, fairness testing might reveal that applicants from a particular ethnic group are systematically denied loans at a higher rate than others. Identifying such biases allows for corrective actions, such as adjusting the training data, modifying decision thresholds, or re-evaluating feature importance.

In addition to fairness audits, adversarial testing can help identify vulnerabilities in a model's decision-making process. Adversarial testing involves stress-testing the model with specially crafted inputs designed to expose weaknesses or inconsistencies. For example, in a facial recognition system, adversarial testing might involve testing the model with slightly altered images to see if it misclassifies certain individuals. This type of testing ensures that the model remains robust and does not produce unpredictable or biased results under different conditions. Regular fairness and robustness assessments help maintain model integrity and trustworthiness over time.

Explainability should not be treated as an afterthought but rather as an integral part of the model development lifecycle. Integrating interpretability tools early in the development process ensures that transparency considerations are incorporated from the beginning rather than being retrofitted later. Data scientists and engineers should design models with interpretability in mind, choosing architectures and algorithms that balance predictive performance with explainability. Throughout the lifecycle of the model, interpretability tools should be continuously applied to monitor how the model evolves and whether its explanations remain valid. This is particularly important in dynamic environments where models are retrained on new data. For instance, in an online recommendation system, user preferences may shift over time, requiring periodic updates to ensure that explanations remain relevant and accurate. Establishing continuous monitoring of model explanations ensures that transparency efforts keep pace with changes in data and model performance.

Adopting regulatory-compliant AI practices is another essential best practice for making models transparent and actionable. In industries such as healthcare, finance, and legal services, strict regulations govern the use of AI and machine learning. Regulatory bodies often require that model decisions be explainable, auditable, and free from bias. Ensuring compliance with explainability requirements involves documenting how the model works, maintaining an audit trail of predictions, and providing clear justifications for decisions. For example, in the financial sector, laws such as the Equal Credit Opportunity Act (ECOA) require lenders to provide applicants with explanations for credit decisions. An AI-driven credit scoring model must be able to generate explanations that satisfy regulatory requirements while also being understandable to customers.

To support regulatory compliance, organizations should implement robust documentation practices that track the entire lifecycle of a machine learning model. This includes recording the sources of training data, documenting feature selection processes, describing the model's architecture, and keeping records of model evaluations. Maintaining an audit trail of model decisions allows for transparency and accountability, making it easier to investigate issues if the model produces unexpected or controversial outcomes. Additionally, organizations should stay informed about emerging AI regulations and ethical guidelines to ensure that their models remain compliant as legal and ethical standards evolve.

By adopting these best practices, organizations can create machine learning models that are not only accurate but also transparent, trustworthy, and aligned with ethical and regulatory expectations. Ensuring that explanations are tailored to different audiences, using model-agnostic interpretability techniques, conducting fairness and bias testing, integrating explainability into the development lifecycle, and adhering to regulatory requirements are all essential steps toward making AI models more transparent and actionable. These efforts contribute to building trust in AI-driven systems and enable organizations to deploy machine learning models responsibly in real-world applications.

The Future of Explainable AI

The future of explainable AI is poised to play a critical role in shaping how artificial intelligence systems are developed, deployed, and trusted. As AI models become more complex, particularly with advancements in deep learning and large-scale models, ensuring transparency and interpretability will be essential for their widespread adoption. AI is increasingly being integrated into high-stakes domains such as healthcare, finance, autonomous systems, and legal decision-making, where understanding how a model arrives at its predictions is crucial for ensuring fairness, accountability, and trustworthiness. This growing need for explainability has led to several emerging trends in research and development aimed at making AI systems more transparent and interpretable.

One of the most promising advancements in the field of explainability is the development of self-explaining AI models. Unlike traditional black-box models that require post-hoc interpretation techniques, self-explaining models are designed with built-in interpretability mechanisms that make their decision-making process inherently transparent. These models integrate interpretability into their architecture, allowing them to generate explanations alongside their predictions. For example, attention-based neural networks, such as transformers used in natural language processing, provide insights into which words or phrases contribute most to a model's decision. Similarly, prototype-based models generate decisions by comparing new inputs to representative examples from the training data, making it easier for users to understand why a particular prediction was made. By embedding interpretability directly into the model, self-explaining AI reduces the reliance on external explanation tools and improves trust in AI-driven systems.

Another significant development in explainable AI is the integration of causal inference techniques. Traditional explainability methods, such as SHAP and LIME, focus on feature importance and correlation-based explanations, but they do not establish true cause-and-effect relationships. Causal inference goes beyond correlation by identifying the underlying factors that directly influence an outcome. This is particularly important in fields such as healthcare, where understanding causal relationships can lead to better treatment recommendations. For instance, in a predictive model for patient outcomes, correlation-based explanations might suggest that a particular medication is associated with lower mortality rates. However, causal inference techniques can determine whether the medication itself is responsible for the improvement or if other confounding factors, such as overall patient health, are at play. By incorporating causal reasoning into AI systems, explainability can move from descriptive insights to actionable, decision-driven explanations that help users make informed choices.

Another major shift in the future of explainable AI is the integration of human-in-the-loop AI systems. As AI becomes more autonomous, there is a growing emphasis on ensuring that humans remain actively involved in decision-making processes. Human-in-the-loop systems allow for real-time interaction between AI models and human users, enabling continuous feedback and adjustments to improve both model performance and interpretability. In these systems, AI generates explanations that are reviewed by human experts, who can then refine the model based on their domain knowledge. This collaborative approach enhances trust in AI by ensuring that model decisions align with human reasoning and ethical considerations. For example, in medical diagnostics, AI models can suggest possible diagnoses, but doctors ultimately make the final decision based on both AI-generated insights and their clinical expertise. By combining machine intelligence with human judgment, explainability becomes more practical and aligned with real-world decision-making.

As AI explainability continues to evolve, organizations that prioritize interpretability will be better positioned to build trust, ensure fairness, and comply with regulatory standards. Regulatory bodies around the world are increasingly emphasizing the need for AI transparency, particularly in sensitive areas such as finance, healthcare, and hiring. The European Union's AI Act, for example, outlines strict requirements for explainability in high-risk AI applications, mandating that organizations provide clear and understandable justifications for automated decisions. Similarly, financial institutions are required to explain credit decisions to consumers under laws such as the Equal Credit Opportunity Act. Companies that proactively invest in explainability frameworks will not only meet regulatory requirements but also differentiate themselves by fostering trust with users and stakeholders.

Beyond regulatory compliance, improving explainability in AI systems will lead to better decision-making and greater adoption of AI technologies. Users are more likely to trust and engage with AI when they can understand how decisions are made. In customer-facing applications, such as AI-powered recommendation systems, providing clear explanations can enhance user experience and satisfaction. For example, an e-commerce recommendation system that explains why certain products are suggested—based on past purchases, browsing history, or user preferences—can increase customer trust and engagement. Similarly, AI-driven hiring platforms that provide transparent explanations for why candidates are shortlisted can improve fairness and reduce concerns about bias in automated recruitment processes.

As AI continues to advance, the next frontier in explainability will likely involve more intuitive and interactive explanation methods. Researchers are exploring new ways to present explanations in ways that are easy to understand for non-technical users, such as through visual storytelling, conversational AI interfaces, and natural language explanations. Instead of presenting users with complex numerical feature importance scores, AI systems may generate explanations in the form of interactive graphs, simulations, or even dialogue-based interfaces where users can ask follow-up questions about the model's decision. This shift towards more user-friendly explainability will make AI more accessible and increase public confidence in automated systems.

Ultimately, the future of explainable AI will be defined by the ability to balance model complexity with transparency, ensuring that AI systems remain both powerful and understandable. The push towards self-explaining models, causal inference techniques, human-in-the-loop AI, and regulatory compliance will drive innovations in explainability, making AI systems more accountable and trustworthy. Organizations that prioritize these advancements will not only build better AI-driven solutions but also foster long-term adoption of artificial intelligence across industries. By embedding transparency into AI from the ground up, the next generation of intelligent systems will be more aligned with human values, ethical considerations, and real-world needs.

8

Scaling Machine Learning Systems

As machine learning models grow in complexity and size, scaling them efficiently becomes a critical challenge. Large-scale machine learning systems must handle vast amounts of data, support high-throughput inference, and ensure seamless deployment in production environments. Scaling involves optimizing model training, improving inference speed, and ensuring robust deployment infrastructure. These challenges are particularly important for deep learning models, recommendation systems, natural language processing (NLP), and real-time AI applications. Achieving efficient scalability requires a combination of distributed computing, hardware acceleration, software optimizations, and effective data engineering.

Scaling Model Training: Optimizing Large-Scale Datasets and Distributed Learning

Scaling model training for large-scale datasets and distributed learning requires optimizing computational resources, improving data processing efficiency, and utilizing parallelization strategies to handle the increasing complexity of modern machine learning models. As datasets grow in size and models become more sophisticated, single-machine training approaches often fail to meet performance demands due to memory constraints and excessive training times. To address these challenges, distributed training techniques, advanced hardware accelerators, and optimized data pipelines have become essential for improving efficiency and scalability in AI training workflows.

One of the fundamental strategies for scaling machine learning training is the use of data parallelism and model parallelism. Data parallelism is a widely used approach where the dataset is divided across multiple GPUs or machines, and each worker processes a different subset of the data. All workers train a copy of the same model on their respective data partitions, and their gradients are synchronized after each iteration to ensure consistency in model updates. This approach is particularly effective for deep learning models where the parameters fit within a single device's memory, allowing multiple GPUs to work together efficiently without overwhelming any individual unit. In contrast, model parallelism involves splitting the model itself across multiple devices, with different layers or components of the neural network allocated to different hardware resources. This method is essential for training extremely large models, such as transformer-based architectures like GPT-4, which exceed the memory capacity of a single GPU. Hybrid strategies combining both data and model parallelism are often employed in large-scale deep learning to maximize efficiency while handling memory limitations.

Distributed training frameworks play a crucial role in enabling scalable and efficient training across multiple machines and hardware accelerators. Horovod, developed by Uber, is one of the most popular frameworks for distributed deep learning. It is built on top of TensorFlow, PyTorch, and MXNet, optimizing gradient aggregation and reducing communication overhead between GPUs. By using ring-allreduce algorithms, Horovod minimizes the latency associated with synchronizing model updates across different devices, making it a preferred choice for high-performance deep learning applications. Another significant optimization library is DeepSpeed, developed by Microsoft, which is designed to improve the efficiency of training large transformer models. DeepSpeed enables optimizations such as zero-redundancy optimizers, which reduce memory consumption by partitioning optimizer states across multiple GPUs, making it possible to train massive models that would otherwise be infeasible due to memory constraints. TensorFlow also provides distributed training strategies, such as MirroredStrategy for synchronous data parallelism and TPUStrategy for leveraging Google's Tensor Processing Units (TPUs), which enable efficient large-scale training with reduced energy consumption.

The role of hardware acceleration in large-scale model training is crucial, as AI workloads require significant computational power. GPUs, particularly NVIDIA's high-performance models such as the A100 and H100, are the industry standard for training deep learning models due to their parallel processing capabilities. TPUs, developed by Google, offer specialized acceleration for neural networks, particularly for workloads running on Google Cloud. In addition to GPUs and TPUs, specialized hardware solutions such as Cerebras Wafer-Scale Engines and Graphcore Intelligence Processing Units (IPUs) are designed to handle AI workloads with extreme parallelism, providing new avenues for high-performance model training. Field-Programmable Gate Arrays (FPGAs) also play a role in AI acceleration, particularly in edge computing applications where low latency and energy efficiency are critical. By leveraging these hardware advancements, AI researchers and engineers can train increasingly large and complex models while optimizing computational efficiency.

Another important consideration in distributed training is the choice between synchronous and asynchronous training. Synchronous training ensures that all workers process the same batch of data before updating model parameters, maintaining consistency across all devices. However, this approach can slow down training if certain workers take longer to process data, causing a bottleneck. Asynchronous training, on the other hand, allows workers to update parameters independently, improving efficiency by enabling faster updates. However, asynchronous training introduces the issue of stale gradients, where some model updates may be based on outdated versions of the parameters. Techniques such as Elastic Averaging Stochastic Gradient Descent (EASGD) and stale gradient correction methods help mitigate this issue by dynamically adjusting the learning process to account for discrepancies in updates. By selecting the appropriate training synchronization method based on model complexity and computational constraints, AI engineers can balance efficiency and consistency in distributed learning.

Optimizing data pipelines is another critical factor in scaling model training for large-scale datasets. Data sharding, which involves partitioning large datasets into smaller chunks that can be processed in parallel, improves data loading efficiency and prevents bottlenecks during training. Prefetching and caching techniques, such as TensorFlow's tf.data API, enable data to be loaded into memory ahead of time, reducing idle time for GPUs and improving overall throughput.

A feature store is another important component of scalable machine learning workflows, providing a centralized repository for preprocessed features that can be reused across different models. By storing engineered features in a standardized format, feature stores reduce redundancy, enhance data consistency, and accelerate model training by eliminating the need to recompute feature transformations for each new training iteration.

The ability to train machine learning models on a scale depends on a combination of distributed training strategies, optimized data pipelines, and hardware acceleration. As AI continues to evolve, the demand for large-scale training will only increase, driving the need for more efficient methods of parallelization and resource allocation. Organizations investing in scalable AI infrastructure will be better equipped to train state-of-the-art models while maintaining efficiency, reducing training costs, and improving deployment readiness. By integrating data parallelism, model parallelism, advanced distributed training frameworks, and high-performance hardware, AI practitioners can build more powerful and scalable machine learning systems that push the boundaries of what is possible in artificial intelligence.

Optimizing Inference: Reducing Latency and Computing Costs

Optimizing inference for machine learning models is essential for reducing latency, minimizing computational costs, and ensuring efficient hardware utilization, particularly in real-time applications. Once a model has been trained, deploying it in production requires fine-tuning to meet performance constraints, as large models with high computational requirements can introduce delays and excessive resource consumption. Techniques such as model quantization, pruning, knowledge distillation, efficient serving architectures, and hardware acceleration play a crucial role in making inference both faster and more efficient.

Model quantization is one of the most effective strategies for reducing inference time and memory usage. Standard machine learning models are typically trained using 32-bit floating point precision, which provides high numerical accuracy but demands significant computational power. Quantization reduces the precision of model weights and activations, often down to 8-bit integers, thereby lowering memory consumption and speeding up inference without a major drop in accuracy. There are two main approaches to quantization: post-training quantization (PTQ) and quantization-aware training (QAT). PTQ applies quantization after training, making it a simpler and faster approach, but it may lead to some loss in accuracy if the model is not well-calibrated. QAT, on the other hand, incorporates quantization into the training process, allowing the model to learn and adapt to lower-precision arithmetic, which helps maintain higher accuracy. Several frameworks facilitate model quantization, including TensorFlow Lite for mobile and embedded systems, ONNX Runtime for cross-platform inference acceleration, and NVIDIA TensorRT for deploying optimized models on GPUs.

Pruning and sparsity are additional techniques that enhance inference efficiency by reducing the number of model parameters while preserving performance. Large deep learning models often contain redundant or less significant parameters that contribute little to overall accuracy. Pruning techniques aim to remove these unnecessary components, thereby reducing model size and speeding up computations. Structured pruning eliminates entire neurons, channels, or filters, making the model more compact and easier to run on specialized hardware. Unstructured pruning removes individual weights, creating sparse matrices that can be processed more efficiently on hardware optimized for sparse computations, such as NVIDIA's Ampere GPUs. By incorporating sparsity, pruned models achieve faster inference speeds and lower memory usage, making them particularly useful for edge AI applications where computational resources are limited.

Knowledge distillation is another approach used to optimize inference by compressing large, complex models into smaller, faster ones while retaining high predictive performance. In this process, a high capacity "teacher" model transfers its knowledge to a more lightweight "student" model, which learns to mimic the teacher's outputs with fewer parameters and computations. This technique is especially useful in deploying models on mobile devices, embedded systems, and cloud applications where computational efficiency is a priority. Examples of knowledge distillation in practice include TinyBERT and DistilBERT, which reduce the size of transformer models while maintaining strong performance in natural language processing tasks. Similarly, MobileNet uses knowledge distillation to create lightweight computer vision models that can run efficiently on mobile devices without sacrificing accuracy.

Efficient serving architectures play a crucial role in optimizing inference by improving request handling and minimizing computational bottlenecks. In production environments, inference requests can arrive at high rates, requiring strategies to optimize response times and throughput. One common approach is batching, where multiple inference requests are processed together rather than individually, increasing computational efficiency. NVIDIA Triton Inference Server supports request batching, allowing deep learning models to handle higher workloads efficiently. Streaming and online inference methods are essential for applications that require continuous predictions, such as fraud detection, recommendation systems, and autonomous driving. Instead of processing data in discrete batches, streaming inference allows models to update predictions in real time, enabling faster decision-making. Another key aspect of serving architectures is edge AI deployment, which involves running models on local edge devices rather than relying on cloud-based inference. Edge deployment reduces latency, enhances privacy, and decreases dependency on internet connectivity. Devices such as NVIDIA Jetson Nano, Google Coral TPUs, and Apple's Neural Engine are specifically designed for efficient on-device AI inference, enabling low-power AI applications in smart cameras, IoT devices, and robotics.

Hardware acceleration is a fundamental aspect of optimizing inference, as specialized hardware significantly enhances performance while reducing computational costs. NVIDIA TensorRT is one of the most widely used inference engines for deploying deep learning models on GPUs. It optimizes neural networks by applying techniques such as layer fusion, reduced precision arithmetic, and kernel auto-tuning, leading to significant speedups in inference performance. Another key framework is ONNX Runtime, which provides cross-platform acceleration by enabling model execution on different hardware backends, including GPUs, CPUs, and FPGAs. The TVM compiler stack further enhances inference performance by optimizing models for diverse hardware architectures, automatically tuning computational graphs to improve efficiency across different processors. By leveraging these hardware acceleration tools, AI practitioners can achieve lower latency and higher throughput, making AI applications more practical for real-world deployment.

Optimizing inference is a crucial step in bringing machine learning models from research to production. By applying techniques such as quantization, pruning, knowledge distillation, and efficient serving architectures, organizations can reduce computational costs while maintaining high model performance. Hardware acceleration further enhances inference efficiency, enabling AI applications to run in real-time with minimal latency. As machine learning models continue to grow in complexity, developing scalable inference solutions will be essential for ensuring their usability in applications ranging from mobile AI to large-scale cloud-based services.

Deploying Scalable Machine Learning Systems in Production

Deploying scalable machine learning systems in production is a critical step that ensures models operate efficiently, reliably, and at scale. Once a model has been trained and optimized for inference, the challenge shifts to integrating it into a production environment where it can serve predictions consistently while adapting to changing data and operational conditions. Achieving this requires robust strategies for containerization, orchestration, model versioning, continuous deployment, monitoring, and scalable cloud deployment.

Containerization is one of the foundational techniques used to streamline model deployment, providing a consistent and portable execution environment. Docker is widely used to package machine learning models along with their dependencies, ensuring that they run the same way across different environments. By encapsulating the model within a container, deployment becomes easier across cloud platforms, on-premise servers, and edge devices. However, as machine learning systems scale, managing multiple containers and distributed workloads becomes complex. This is where orchestration tools like Kubernetes come into play. Kubernetes automates the deployment, scaling, and management of containerized applications, allowing AI workloads to be efficiently distributed across multiple nodes in a cloud or on-premises cluster. To further optimize machine learning workflows, Kubeflow, an extension of Kubernetes designed for AI applications, provides capabilities for training, serving, and monitoring models in a scalable manner.

Model versioning and continuous deployment are essential for ensuring that machine learning models remain reproducible, up to date, and easy to roll back if necessary. Machine learning models are not static; they evolve over time as data distributions shift and new training iterations improve performance. Tools like MLflow, DVC (Data Version Control), and ModelDB allow teams to track different versions of a model, storing metadata, training parameters, and performance metrics. This ensures that teams can compare models, reproduce previous results, and manage deployments effectively. Continuous Integration and Continuous Deployment (CI/CD) pipelines for machine learning, often referred to as MLOps, automate the entire lifecycle of a model, from data preprocessing and training to validation and deployment. Frameworks like TensorFlow Extended (TFX) and AWS SageMaker Pipelines enable teams to automate workflows, ensuring that models are continuously trained and deployed based on new data. These pipelines also incorporate automated validation steps to prevent underperforming models from being deployed, reducing the risk of degraded performance in production.

Monitoring deployed models is crucial to detect issues such as model drift, data quality problems, and performance degradation over time. Real-world data distributions change, and models that once performed well may become less effective as new patterns emerge. Model drift detection mechanisms track deviations in input data and predictions, triggering alerts or automatic retraining when necessary. A/B testing is another critical approach that allows teams to deploy multiple models simultaneously and compare their performance on live data before committing to a full rollout. By routing a portion of incoming requests to different model versions, organizations can collect real-world performance data and ensure that new models provide meaningful improvements before completely replacing older ones. Observability tools such as Prometheus, Grafana, and the ELK Stack (Elasticsearch, Logstash, Kibana) help teams monitor model behavior in real time, providing dashboards and alerting mechanisms to identify anomalies, latency issues, or unexpected shifts in prediction patterns.

Scalable cloud deployment enables machine learning models to serve predictions efficiently across diverse environments. Cloud platforms such as AWS SageMaker, Google Vertex AI, and Azure Machine Learning provide managed services for deploying and scaling models, reducing the operational burden on engineering teams. These platforms offer built-in model hosting, automatic scaling, and integration with monitoring and logging tools. Serverless AI architectures further optimize cloud deployments by allowing models to be executed in an event-driven manner, eliminating the need for always-on infrastructure. Services like AWS Lambda and Google Cloud Functions enable inference to be triggered dynamically, reducing costs by only using computing resources when needed. This approach is particularly useful for applications with sporadic inference demands, such as fraud detection or chatbots that only process user requests intermittently.

Federated learning and privacy-preserving AI techniques are becoming increasingly important in scenarios where data privacy and security are critical concerns. Traditional machine learning workflows require centralizing data for training, which can pose significant privacy risks, especially in industries such as healthcare, finance, and telecommunications. Federated learning addresses this challenge by training models directly on decentralized devices, such as smartphones or edge servers, without transmitting sensitive data to a central repository. This technique has been successfully implemented by companies like Google, which uses federated learning to improve the predictive capabilities of its Gboard keyboard without compromising user privacy. In addition to federated learning, techniques like differential privacy and homomorphic encryption enable AI models to learn from sensitive data without exposing it. Differential privacy introduces controlled noise into the training data, ensuring that individual data points cannot be traced back while still allowing meaningful patterns to be extracted. Homomorphic encryption goes a step further by allowing computations to be performed directly on encrypted data, ensuring that sensitive information remains confidential throughout the entire inference process.

Deploying scalable machine learning systems requires a combination of efficient infrastructure management, automated model lifecycle tracking, real-time monitoring, and privacy-conscious deployment strategies. By leveraging containerization with Docker, orchestration with Kubernetes, model versioning tools, MLOps pipelines, cloud-based inference services, and federated learning techniques, organizations can ensure that their machine learning models operate efficiently, adapt to evolving data, and comply with security and privacy requirements. As AI adoption continues to grow, mastering these deployment strategies will be essential for building reliable and scalable machine learning solutions that deliver real-world impact.

Building Scalable and Efficient ML Systems

Building scalable and efficient machine learning systems is a complex process that involves optimizing every stage of the machine learning lifecycle, from data processing and model training to inference and deployment. As organizations increasingly rely on AI to drive decision-making and automation, ensuring that models can handle large-scale data, operate efficiently on various hardware architectures, and integrate seamlessly into production environments is crucial. The key challenge lies in balancing computational performance, cost efficiency, and interpretability while maintaining robustness and adaptability to real-world data shifts.

One of the most critical aspects of scaling machine learning systems is distributed training, which allows models to be trained on massive datasets without being constrained by the memory and processing limitations of a single machine. Distributed training can be implemented using two primary approaches: data parallelism and model parallelism. In data parallelism, the dataset is split across multiple computing nodes, with each node training an identical copy of the model on different subsets of data and synchronizing gradients during backpropagation. This approach is widely used for deep learning models, where all model parameters can fit within a single GPU or TPU, but the dataset size is too large for a single device to handle efficiently. In contrast, model parallelism divides the model itself across multiple devices, with different parts of the network assigned to different computational resources. This is particularly useful for extremely large neural networks, such as transformer-based models like GPT-4, where a single GPU lacks sufficient memory to store all parameters. Many large-scale machines learning frameworks, including TensorFlow, PyTorch, and JAX, offer built-in support for distributed training through libraries such as Horovod, DeepSpeed, and TensorFlow Distributed Strategies.

Efficient hardware utilization is another key factor in scaling machine learning systems. Traditional CPUs, while effective for certain workloads, are often insufficient for the computational demands of deep learning. Instead, specialized hardware accelerators such as GPUs, TPUs, FPGAs, and AI-specific chips like Cerebras Wafer-Scale Engine or Graphcore IPUs provide significant speedups for training and inference. Modern AI workloads leverage techniques such as mixed-precision training, which reduces memory usage and increases computational efficiency by using lower-precision floating-point formats (e.g., FP16 instead of FP32) without sacrificing model accuracy. Additionally, hardware-aware optimization libraries like NVIDIA TensorRT and OpenVINO help fine-tune model execution for specific chip architectures, further improving performance.

Model compression techniques play a crucial role in making machine learning systems more efficient, especially for deployment in resource-constrained environments such as edge devices and mobile applications. Quantization is one of the most widely used compression methods, reducing model size and inference latency by converting high-precision floating-point weights into lower-bit representations like INT8 or even binary formats. Post-training quantization (PTQ) and quantization-aware training (QAT) enable models to maintain high accuracy while benefiting from reduced memory footprints and faster execution speeds. Pruning is another important compression strategy, where redundant or low-impact weights are removed from the model to reduce its size and improve inference speed. Structured pruning eliminates entire neurons or convolutional filters, while unstructured pruning removes individual weights based on their significance. Knowledge distillation is yet another effective technique, where a large, complex model (the teacher) transfers its learned knowledge to a smaller, more efficient model (the student), retaining most of the predictive power while significantly reducing computational costs.

Deploying machine learning models at scale requires robust and automated pipelines to handle continuous integration, monitoring, and retraining. The field of MLOps, which applies DevOps principles to machine learning, has become essential for managing AI workflows efficiently. MLOps frameworks like MLflow, Kubeflow, and TensorFlow Extended (TFX) provide versioning, tracking, and deployment capabilities that ensure models remain reproducible and easy to update. Continuous deployment pipelines automate the process of retraining models when new data becomes available, validating them against predefined benchmarks, and rolling them out into production with minimal human intervention. Monitoring is equally important to detect model drift, data anomalies, and performance degradation. Real-time monitoring tools such as Prometheus, Grafana, and Amazon SageMaker Model Monitor help organizations track prediction accuracy, latency, and data distribution changes, allowing them to take corrective actions when necessary.

Federated learning is emerging as a powerful approach to scaling machine learning while preserving data privacy. Traditional machine learning workflows require centralizing data for training, which can introduce privacy risks, regulatory challenges, and high data transfer costs. Federated learning enables AI models to be trained across decentralized devices, such as smartphones or IoT sensors, without requiring raw data to be sent to a central server. This approach is particularly useful in applications such as personalized recommendation systems, healthcare diagnostics, and financial fraud detection, where user data must remain confidential. By aggregating model updates instead of raw data, federated learning ensures privacy while leveraging the collective knowledge of distributed datasets. Techniques such as differential privacy and secure multi-party computation further enhance data security by ensuring that no individual data point can be traced back during model training or inference.

Hardware acceleration for inference is another critical factor in scaling AI systems, as real-time applications such as autonomous driving, speech recognition, and financial trading require ultra-low latency predictions. Optimized inference engines like NVIDIA TensorRT, ONNX Runtime, and TVM Compiler Stack enable machine learning models to execute efficiently across different hardware platforms. Edge AI deployment is gaining traction, with companies deploying AI models directly on low-power devices such as Jetson Nano, Google Coral TPUs, and Apple's Neural Engine to minimize latency and reduce reliance on cloud-based inference. By processing data locally, edge AI solutions not only improve response times but also reduce bandwidth costs and enhance privacy.

Looking ahead, advances in AI hardware, software frameworks, and model architectures will continue to push the boundaries of scalability and efficiency in machine learning. The development of self-supervised learning techniques, more efficient neural network architectures, and energy-efficient AI chips will further optimize AI workflows. Organizations that invest in scalable AI infrastructure, robust MLOps pipelines, and privacy-preserving technologies will be better positioned to deploy powerful and cost-effective AI solutions. As machine learning systems become increasingly integrated into critical business operations, ensuring that they remain interpretable, adaptive, and efficient will be essential for maximizing their long-term impact and usability.

9

Ethics and biases in Machine Learning

Machine learning models are becoming deeply embedded in societal decision-making processes, shaping outcomes in critical areas such as employment, finance, healthcare, and criminal justice. While these models offer efficiency and predictive power, they also introduce ethical challenges that must be carefully managed to ensure fairness, transparency, and accountability. The consequences of biased or opaque models can be severe, leading to systemic discrimination, economic disparities, and erosion of public trust in AI systems. Addressing these challenges requires a comprehensive approach that integrates ethical AI design, rigorous model evaluation, regulatory oversight, and active stakeholder engagement.

Bias in machine learning models arises from multiple sources, including biased training data, algorithmic design flaws, and historical inequalities embedded in real-world data. When AI systems are trained on datasets that reflect existing societal biases, they can learn and amplify these patterns, leading to unfair outcomes. For example, hiring algorithms trained on historical employment data may favor male candidates if past hiring decisions were biased against women. Similarly, predictive policing models trained on crime data may disproportionately target minority communities due to historical over-policing in those areas. Bias can also emerge from feature selection, where certain variables serve as proxies for sensitive attributes such as race, gender, or socioeconomic status, inadvertently leading to discriminatory predictions. To mitigate bias, AI developers must adopt techniques such as debiasing algorithms, adversarial training, and fairness-aware machine learning that actively counteract disparities in model predictions.

Transparency is another critical concern in AI ethics, as many machine learning models, especially deep learning systems, operate as black boxes, making it difficult to understand how they arrive at specific decisions. Lack of transparency can lead to distrust, particularly in high-stakes applications where individuals are affected by automated decisions without clear explanations. Explainable AI (XAI) techniques, such as SHAP (Shapley Additive Explanations) and LIME (Local Interpretable Model-agnostic Explanations), help shed light on model decision-making by identifying key features that influence predictions. In fields like healthcare and finance, regulatory frameworks increasingly demand that AI-driven decisions be interpretable and justifiable. For instance, the General Data Protection Regulation (GDPR) in the European Union includes a "right to explanation," requiring organizations to provide understandable reasons for automated decisions that impact individuals. Developing AI systems with built-in explainability ensures that stakeholders—including regulators, domain experts, and affected users—can scrutinize and challenge AI-driven outcomes.

Accountability in AI involves establishing mechanisms to hold developers, organizations, and policymakers responsible for the ethical implications of machine learning systems. One of the primary challenges in AI accountability is the "responsibility gap," where it is unclear who should be held liable when AI systems make harmful or unethical decisions. For example, if an autonomous vehicle causes an accident, responsibility may be distributed across multiple parties, including software developers, data providers, and manufacturers. To address this challenge, organizations must implement rigorous auditing processes that track decision-making pathways and identify potential risks before deployment. Algorithmic impact assessments (AIAs) are gaining traction as a tool to evaluate the societal and ethical implications of AI models before they are put into practice. These assessments involve evaluating potential biases, testing for disparate impacts on different demographic groups, and ensuring compliance with legal and ethical standards.

Beyond individual model evaluations, regulatory oversight is essential to ensure that AI systems adhere to ethical guidelines and legal requirements. Governments and regulatory bodies worldwide are developing AI governance frameworks to establish standards for fairness, transparency, and accountability. The European Union's AI Act, for instance, categorizes AI applications into different risk levels, imposing stricter regulations on high-risk systems such as biometric surveillance, credit scoring, and automated hiring tools. Similarly, in the United States, agencies like the Federal Trade Commission (FTC) and the National Institute of Standards and Technology (NIST) are developing guidelines to promote ethical AI practices in commercial and governmental applications. Industry-led initiatives, such as

Google's AI Principles and Microsoft's Responsible AI framework, also play a role in setting ethical standards for AI deployment. However, regulatory frameworks must strike a balance between fostering innovation and preventing the misuse of AI technologies. Overly restrictive regulations could hinder technological progress, while insufficient oversight could allow harmful AI applications to proliferate unchecked.

Active stakeholder engagement is crucial for developing AI systems that align with societal values and ethical norms. This involves including diverse perspectives in AI development, from data scientists and ethicists to community representatives and civil rights advocates. Participatory AI design approaches encourage collaboration between technical experts and affected communities to ensure that AI models serve the needs of all users fairly. For example, organizations developing AI-powered hiring tools can work directly with labor rights groups to identify potential biases and ensure that hiring algorithms promote diversity and inclusion. Public consultation processes, such as AI ethics advisory boards and open forums, provide additional opportunities for transparency and accountability by allowing stakeholders to voice concerns and contribute to ethical decision-making.

The broader societal impact of automated decision-making extends beyond individual fairness concerns to issues such as economic inequality, labor displacement, and surveillance risks. As AI systems become more pervasive, there is a growing need to assess their long-term consequences on employment and social structures. Automation has the potential to displace jobs, particularly in industries reliant on routine cognitive and manual tasks. Policymakers must proactively address these challenges by investing in workforce retraining programs, ensuring that AI-driven economic growth benefits all sectors of society. Additionally, the rise of AI-driven surveillance technologies raises concerns about privacy and civil liberties. Governments and corporations deploying facial recognition and predictive policing systems must ensure that these technologies do not disproportionately target marginalized communities or erode fundamental rights.

Understanding Bias in Machine Learning

Bias in machine learning arises when models systematically favor or disadvantage certain groups, leading to unfair outcomes. This bias can emerge from multiple sources, including the data used for training, the underlying algorithms, and the human decisions that shape the model development process. Since machine learning systems are trained on real-world data, they often inherit and reinforce historical inequalities, making it essential to identify and mitigate bias to ensure fair and ethical AI applications.

One major source of bias in machine learning is historical bias, which occurs when training data reflects pre-existing societal inequalities. For instance, facial recognition systems have been shown to perform more accurately on lighter-skinned individuals compared to darker-skinned individuals because they are often trained on datasets that predominantly contain images of people with lighter skin tones. This leads to higher misidentification rates for individuals from underrepresented groups, reinforcing discrimination in applications such as law enforcement and security. Similarly, hiring algorithms trained on past employment data may favor male candidates if historical hiring practices have disadvantaged women, thereby perpetuating gender imbalances in the workforce.

Another common source of bias is sampling bias, which occurs when certain demographic groups are underrepresented in the training dataset. If a medical AI system is trained primarily on health data from men, it may fail to detect conditions that disproportionately affect women. This can result in misdiagnoses or delayed treatments, particularly in cases where symptoms present differently across genders. Sampling bias also affects recommendation systems, where content or job recommendations may be skewed towards the preferences of the dominant group in the dataset, limiting exposure to diverse opportunities and viewpoints.

Algorithmic bias is another factor that can amplify disparities in machine learning models. Certain algorithms prioritize accuracy as their primary optimization goal, which can lead to unintended consequences for minority groups. In classification tasks, models trained to maximize overall accuracy may disproportionately favor majority groups, as they are overrepresented in the training data. This can lead to unfair treatment in applications such as credit scoring, where minority groups may be unfairly denied loans due to biased model predictions. Additionally, some machine learning techniques, such as deep learning and reinforcement learning, rely on complex decision-making processes that make it difficult to detect and correct biases within the model.

Label bias also plays a significant role in shaping model outcomes, particularly in areas where human annotation is required. In sentiment analysis, for example, training data labeled by human annotators may reflect societal stereotypes and subjective judgments. If annotators consistently associate certain dialects or linguistic patterns with negative sentiment, the resulting model may disproportionately classify text from certain cultural groups as negative, reinforcing harmful stereotypes. Label bias is also prevalent in automated hiring tools, where historical hiring decisions influence the labeling process. If past hiring managers exhibited biases against women or minorities in tech roles, a model trained on this data will learn to replicate and perpetuate those biases in future hiring recommendations.

Proxy bias occurs when seemingly neutral features act as indirect indicators of sensitive attributes such as race, gender, or socioeconomic status. For example, a model predicting loan approvals may consider ZIP codes as a feature, but since residential areas are often segregated along racial and economic lines, ZIP codes may indirectly encode racial bias. This can result in discriminatory lending practices where individuals from historically disadvantaged communities are less likely to receive loans, even if they have similar financial qualifications as individuals from more privileged areas. Proxy bias is particularly concerning AI-driven decision-making, as it can be difficult to detect and often operates in subtle ways that reinforce existing inequalities.

Addressing bias in machine learning requires a commitment to fairness, which can be defined in multiple ways depending on the context. One common fairness definition is demographic parity, which ensures that positive outcomes are distributed equally across different demographic groups. In loan approval models, for instance, demographic parity would require that men and women receive loans at similar rates, assuming they have comparable qualifications. However, demographic parity alone may not be sufficient, as it does not account for differences in underlying risk factors or qualifications.

Another fairness concept is equalized odds, which requires that models have equal false positive and false negative rates across different groups. This ensures that no group is disproportionately impacted by incorrect predictions. In healthcare applications, equalized odds would mean that a diagnostic AI system has the same likelihood of misdiagnosing a condition for different racial or gender groups, preventing disparities in medical treatment. However, achieving equalized odds can be challenging, as it may require sacrificing overall model accuracy to ensure balanced error rates across populations.

Individual fairness is another approach that focuses on ensuring that similar individuals receive similar predictions, regardless of group identity. This approach emphasizes treating people based on their actual characteristics rather than group membership. For instance, in a hiring algorithm, two candidates with nearly identical skills and experience should receive similar recommendations, regardless of gender or race. Individual fairness helps ensure that AI decisions are based on merit rather than biased patterns learned from historical data.

Ultimately, mitigating bias in machine learning requires a combination of ethical AI design, diverse and representative training data, fairness-aware algorithms, and ongoing monitoring of model behavior. Techniques such as adversarial debiasing, re-weighting training samples, and fairness constraints in optimization algorithms can help create more equitable models. Additionally, regulatory frameworks and ethical guidelines play a crucial role in enforcing fairness standards and ensuring that AI systems do not reinforce societal inequalities. As machine learning continues to influence critical decision-making processes, addressing bias and ensuring fairness will remain essential to building trustworthy and ethical AI systems.

Accountability in AI Systems

AI accountability ensures that machine learning models operate in an ethical, transparent, and fair manner, requiring organizations and developers to take responsibility for their AI systems. As AI increasingly influences decisions in areas such as hiring, healthcare, finance, and law enforcement, accountability becomes essential to prevent harm, discrimination, and misuse. A comprehensive approach to AI accountability involves strategies such as explainability, transparency, human oversight, and bias mitigation.

One of the foundational elements of AI accountability is explainability and transparency. AI models, particularly deep learning models, often function as "black boxes," making it difficult to understand how they arrive at specific predictions. This lack of interpretability can erode trust and make it challenging to detect biases or errors. To address this, interpretable AI models and techniques are used to provide insights into model decision-making. Methods like decision trees, SHAP (Shapley Additive Explanations), and LIME (Local Interpretable Model-agnostic Explanations) allow users to examine the contribution of different features in a model's prediction process. For example, in a loan approval model, SHAP values can highlight whether income, credit score, or past loan defaults had the most impact on the decision.

Model documentation also plays a critical role in ensuring transparency. Frameworks like Google's Model Cards and Datasheets for Datasets provide structured documentation detailing how AI models are trained, validated, and tested, including information on potential biases and limitations. Model Cards, for instance, outline key details such as the intended use cases, performance metrics across different demographic groups, and any known ethical concerns. By making this information accessible, organizations enable stakeholders, including regulators, users, and researchers—to assess the risks and benefits of AI systems before deployment.

Open-source audits further enhance transparency by allowing independent researchers and advocacy groups to examine AI models and datasets. When companies release their models and training data to the public, it enables external experts to conduct fairness assessments, detect biases, and propose improvements. Open-source initiatives have led to the discovery of biases in high-profile AI applications, such as facial recognition systems that exhibit racial disparities in accuracy. While full transparency may not always be possible due to proprietary concerns, organizations can still allow third-party audits under confidentiality agreements to ensure ethical AI practices.

Beyond technical transparency, human oversight and governance are crucial for AI accountability. Organizations should establish ethical AI committees or advisory boards responsible for reviewing the deployment of machine learning models. These committees should include a diverse range of stakeholders, including ethicists, legal experts, data scientists, and representatives from affected communities. By incorporating multiple perspectives, organizations can better anticipate potential harms and implement safeguards to mitigate unintended consequences.

Regulatory compliance also plays a significant role in enforcing accountability. Governments and international organizations have introduced policies such as the EU AI Act, GDPR (General Data Protection Regulation), and the Algorithmic Accountability Act in the United States to regulate AI systems, particularly those that impact human rights and societal well-being. Compliance with these regulations requires organizations to conduct risk assessments, ensure data protection, and provide mechanisms for individuals to challenge AI-driven decisions. For instance, under GDPR, individuals have the right to an explanation for automated decisions that significantly impact them, such as credit scoring or hiring outcomes. Failure to comply with such regulations can result in legal penalties, making it imperative for businesses to align their AI practices with ethical and legal standards.

Auditing pipelines are another essential component of AI accountability. Regular bias audits help organizations detect and address algorithmic discrimination before deployment. Tools such as IBM AI Fairness 360 and Google's What-If Tool enable developers to analyze how their models perform across different demographic groups and identify disparities in outcomes. For example, an audit of a hiring algorithm might reveal that the model disproportionately favors male candidates over female candidates. By conducting periodic audits, companies can make necessary adjustments to their models and ensure they adhere to fairness guidelines.

To mitigate bias in AI systems, organizations must adopt a range of techniques across different stages of model development. Pre-processing methods focus on reducing bias before training begins. One approach is re-weighting training data so that underrepresented groups receive greater consideration in the learning process. Another method is oversampling, where additional synthetic data points are generated for minority groups to balance the dataset. Synthetic Minority Over-sampling Technique (SMOTE), for example, creates artificial examples of underrepresented classes to improve model generalization.

In-processing methods address bias during model training. These techniques modify the training process itself to promote fairness. One common approach is incorporating fairness constraints into the optimization function, ensuring that the model does not disproportionately disadvantage certain groups. Adversarial debiasing is another method, where an auxiliary network is trained alongside the main model to detect and penalize biased outcomes. This technique forces the model to make predictions that are not influenced by sensitive attributes such as race or gender.

Post-processing methods involve adjusting model outputs to ensure equitable outcomes after training. If a model produces biased predictions, post-processing techniques can recalibrate the decision thresholds for different demographic groups. For instance, in a loan approval system, if the model's threshold for approving loans is higher for women than for men, post-processing can adjust it to ensure equal opportunity. While post-processing can be effective, it is often seen as a last resort, as it does not address the root causes of bias within the model itself.

Ultimately, AI accountability requires a holistic approach that combines technical solutions, governance structures, regulatory compliance, and continuous monitoring. As AI systems become more prevalent, organizations must prioritize ethical considerations to prevent harm, build public trust, and ensure that their models serve all individuals fairly. By implementing transparent and interpretable models, maintaining rigorous oversight, and actively working to mitigate bias, organizations can create AI systems that are not only powerful but also responsible and equitable.

Societal Impact of AI and Machine Learning

The societal impact of artificial intelligence and machine learning is profound, shaping industries, influencing governance, and redefining human interactions. As AI systems become more advanced and widespread, their effects on employment, privacy, criminal justice, healthcare, and information integrity must be critically examined to ensure ethical and responsible deployment.

AI-driven automation has significantly altered the job market, replacing repetitive, manual tasks with machine-based solutions while simultaneously creating new opportunities in emerging fields. Sectors such as manufacturing, retail, and customer service have seen substantial workforce reductions due to robotic process automation and AI-powered virtual assistants. At the same time, AI has led to the expansion of roles in data science, AI engineering, and ethics-focused technology governance. The challenge lies in ensuring a smooth transition for displaced workers by investing in reskilling and upskilling programs. Governments and corporations must take proactive steps to support career transitions, ensuring that the benefits of automation do not come at the cost of large-scale unemployment. Additionally, AI in hiring presents another critical concern, as biased algorithms can perpetuate discrimination against marginalized groups. Machine learning models trained on biased historical hiring data can reinforce existing prejudices, favoring certain demographics while disadvantaging others. Ensuring fairness in automated hiring requires diverse and representative training datasets, rigorous bias detection techniques, and human oversight to prevent AI from making discriminatory hiring decisions.

Privacy concerns have also emerged as AI systems increasingly rely on large-scale data collection. From facial recognition technologies to consumer behavior tracking, AI has enabled governments and corporations to gather and analyze vast amounts of personal information, often without explicit user consent. Surveillance systems powered by AI have raised ethical questions about mass monitoring, particularly in authoritarian regimes where such technology is used to suppress dissent and restrict individual freedoms. Regulatory oversight and transparency in data collection practices are essential to prevent AI from becoming a tool for unwarranted surveillance. Techniques such as differential privacy, federated learning, and homomorphic encryption can help mitigate privacy risks by enabling AI models to learn from aggregated insights without exposing individual data points. These approaches ensure that AI-driven analytics do not compromise user privacy while still delivering valuable insights for businesses and policymakers.

In criminal justice, AI models are increasingly used to predict crime patterns, assess risks, and even recommend sentencing decisions. However, predictive policing systems have been widely criticized for reinforcing systemic biases present in historical crime data. If a model is trained on biased policing records, it may disproportionately target certain communities, leading to unfair law enforcement practices. The lack of transparency in how these models are developed and evaluated exacerbates the problem, as affected individuals have little recourse to challenge AI-driven decisions. Ensuring fairness in criminal justice applications requires rigorous auditing of AI models, diverse training datasets that do not reflect existing biases, and independent oversight mechanisms to assess the ethical implications of AI-driven policing.

In healthcare, AI has the potential to revolutionize diagnostics, treatment planning, and patient care. Machine learning models trained on medical data can detect diseases at an early stage, recommend personalized treatment plans, and enhance drug discovery. However, the effectiveness of healthcare AI systems is highly dependent on the quality and diversity of their training data. If a model is trained primarily on data from a specific demographic group, it may produce inaccurate diagnoses or treatment recommendations for underrepresented populations. For instance, dermatology AI models trained mostly in images of lighter-skinned individuals have been found to perform poorly in diagnosing skin conditions in darker-skinned patients. To ensure equitable healthcare outcomes, AI models must be trained on diverse datasets that reflect variations in genetic backgrounds, environmental factors, and social determinants of health. Regulatory bodies must also establish guidelines to validate AI models across different population groups before they are deployed in clinical settings.

One of the most alarming consequences of AI advancements is the rise of deepfakes and misinformation. Generative AI technologies have made it increasingly easy to create realistic but entirely fabricated images, videos, and audio recordings. Deepfake videos have been used for malicious purposes, from political disinformation campaigns to fraudulent activities and personal defamation. The proliferation of AI-generated misinformation undermines public trust in digital content, making it difficult to distinguish between truth and manipulation. Addressing this challenge requires a multi-stakeholder approach involving researchers, technology companies, and policymakers. AI-driven detection algorithms can help identify deepfake content, but these tools must evolve alongside generative models to remain effective. Additionally, regulatory measures must be implemented to hold creators and distributors of deceptive AI-generated content accountable. Social media platforms play a crucial role in mitigating the spread of misinformation by improving content moderation strategies, flagging AI-generated content, and promoting media literacy among users.

The widespread adoption of AI and machine learning has the potential to bring significant benefits, but it also introduces ethical and societal risks that must be carefully managed. The challenge lies in balancing innovation with responsibility, ensuring that AI serves humanity without exacerbating existing inequalities or infringing on fundamental rights. By prioritizing ethical AI development, promoting transparency, implementing robust regulations, and fostering public awareness, society can harness the power of AI while safeguarding against its unintended consequences.

Building Ethical and Fair AI Systems

Building ethical and fair AI systems requires a comprehensive and proactive approach that goes beyond technical solutions to encompass social, legal, and organizational considerations. Ensuring that artificial intelligence operates fairly and without bias is not merely a question of refining algorithms but of fundamentally rethinking how AI is designed, trained, deployed, and monitored. Achieving this goal demands the active involvement of diverse stakeholders, including researchers, policymakers, civil society organizations, and the broader public.

One of the most crucial factors in mitigating bias in AI is ensuring that training data is diverse and representative. Machine learning models learn patterns from the data they are trained on, meaning any biases present in that data will be inherited and potentially amplified by the model. Historical biases embedded in datasets can lead to unfair outcomes, reinforcing existing societal inequalities. For instance, if a facial recognition model is trained predominantly on lighter-skinned individuals, it may perform poorly on darker-skinned faces, leading to disparities in accuracy. Similarly, a hiring algorithm trained on historical employment data that reflects gender biases may continue to favor male candidates for certain roles. To address these issues, datasets must be curated with careful attention to diversity, ensuring they include balanced representations of different demographics, socioeconomic backgrounds, and perspectives. This requires collaboration between data scientists and domain experts who can identify potential sources of bias and develop strategies to mitigate them. Additionally, synthetic data generation and techniques such as data reweighting can be used to balance datasets when real-world data is skewed or limited.

Beyond the data itself, fairness-aware algorithms play a critical role in reducing bias in machine learning models. Traditional AI models optimize for accuracy, often at the expense of fairness. However, newer approaches integrate fairness constraints directly into model training, ensuring that outcomes are equitable across different groups. Techniques such as adversarial debiasing train models to minimize differences in predictions across demographic categories, preventing certain groups from being systematically disadvantaged. Other methods, such as equalized odds or demographic parity constraints, ensure that false positive and false negative rates are comparable across subpopulations. While these fairness-aware approaches introduce trade-offs—sometimes reducing overall accuracy to achieve greater equity—they are essential for preventing discriminatory outcomes in high-stakes applications such as credit scoring, healthcare, and criminal justice.

Even with robust data collection and fairness-aware algorithms, AI systems must be continuously monitored and audited for bias over time. Machine learning models do not remain static; they evolve as they interact with real-world data, which can shift in ways that introduce new biases. A system that was initially fair may become biased over time due to concept drift, where the statistical properties of input data change. Continuous monitoring and bias audits are therefore necessary to detect and mitigate biases as they emerge. Organizations can implement fairness dashboards that track key performance metrics across demographic groups, allowing them to identify disparities and take corrective action when necessary. Regular audits using tools such as IBM AI Fairness 360 or Google's What-If Tool enable developers to test models against fairness benchmarks, ensuring they meet ethical standards. Transparency in auditing processes is also critical; companies should openly share their methodologies for assessing fairness and be willing to undergo external reviews to build trust with the public.

Public awareness and education are also essential components of ethical AI development. AI is not created in isolation—it is shaped by human decisions at every stage, from data collection to model design to deployment. As such, AI practitioners must be well-versed in ethical considerations, understanding the societal impact of their work beyond technical performance metrics. Incorporating ethics training into AI education programs can help instill a culture of responsibility among developers and data scientists. At the same time, the general public must also be equipped with the knowledge to critically evaluate AI systems and their implications. When people understand how AI decisions are made, they are better positioned to demand accountability from organizations deploying these technologies. Transparency initiatives such as model documentation frameworks, including Google's Model Cards and Datasheets for Datasets, help bridge the gap between AI developers and end users by providing clear, accessible explanations of how AI systems work and their potential limitations.

Regulatory compliance and legal oversight further reinforce the ethical deployment of AI. Governments around the world are beginning to implement AI regulations aimed at protecting individuals from biased and harmful AI-driven decisions. The European Union's AI Act, for example, categorizes AI applications by risk level and imposes stricter requirements on high-risk systems, such as those used in hiring, banking, and law enforcement. In the United States, the Algorithmic Accountability Act seeks to increase transparency in automated decision-making, requiring companies to conduct impact assessments on their AI systems. Compliance with these regulations not only ensures legal accountability but also fosters trust in AI applications by demonstrating a commitment to fairness and ethical responsibility. However, regulatory frameworks must be continuously updated to keep pace with the rapid advancements in AI technology, and global coordination will be necessary to address ethical concerns in cross-border AI deployments.

Ethical AI is not just a technical challenge; it is a societal issue that requires ongoing collaboration across disciplines. As AI continues to shape the way people work, interact, and make decisions, ensuring fairness, accountability, and transparency becomes more critical than ever. Ethical AI design must be embedded into every stage of the machine learning lifecycle, from data collection and algorithm development to deployment and continuous monitoring. Implementing fairness-aware machine learning practices, regulatory compliance, and public engagement will be key to building trustworthy AI systems that serve all individuals equally. By taking a proactive approach to addressing bias and ethical concerns, organizations can create AI solutions that not only drive innovation but also promote justice and inclusivity in society.

10

Continuous Learning and Model Maintenance

Machine learning models do not exist in static environments; they operate in dynamic ecosystems where data distributions, user behaviors, and business requirements evolve over time. A model that performs well at the time of deployment may experience performance degradation as real-world conditions change. This phenomenon, often referred to as model drift, necessitates continuous learning and maintenance to ensure that AI systems remain accurate, reliable, and aligned with their intended objectives. Maintaining machine learning models in production is not just about occasional retraining; it involves a comprehensive strategy that includes monitoring, data pipeline management, retraining methodologies, and deployment automation.

One of the primary reasons machine learning models degrade over time is data drift, which occurs when the statistical properties of incoming data differ from those used during training. Data drift can be caused by shifts in consumer preferences, economic fluctuations, seasonal trends, or broader societal changes. For example, a recommendation system trained in past user behaviors may struggle to make relevant suggestions if consumer interests shift due to a cultural or economic shift. Another form of drift, concept drift, occurs when the relationship between input features and the target variable changes. In fraud detection, for instance, cybercriminals continually evolve their tactics, making historical fraud patterns less relevant. Without continuous adaptation, a fraud detection model trained on old patterns may fail to recognize new fraudulent activities.

To address these challenges, continuous model monitoring is essential. Organizations must establish robust monitoring pipelines that track key performance indicators (KPIs) such as accuracy, precision, recall, and F1-score in real time. A drop in performance metrics can signal potential model drift, prompting the need for investigation and retraining. Additionally, monitoring should include fairness and bias assessments to ensure that models continue to make equitable decisions as data distributions change. Automated alerting systems can notify data scientists when significant shifts in model behavior are detected, allowing for timely intervention.

Beyond monitoring, effective data pipeline management is critical for maintaining high-quality inputs to machine learning models. Data pipelines must be designed to handle evolving data sources, ensuring that new data is continuously ingested, cleaned, and processed for model updates. Data versioning tools like DVC (Data Version Control) help track changes in datasets, ensuring that updates are reproducible and auditable. Maintaining high-quality labeled data is also a challenge, particularly in supervised learning applications where human annotations are required. Active learning strategies can help by selecting the most informative samples for labeling, reducing the manual effort required for retraining while maximizing performance improvements.

When it comes to updating models, organizations must determine the most effective retraining strategies. There are multiple approaches to continuous learning, each suited to different scenarios. Periodic retraining involves updating models at scheduled intervals, such as weekly or monthly, using the most recent data. This approach works well when data changes gradually over time. However, in highly dynamic environments, retraining must be more adaptive. Online learning techniques enable models to learn incrementally from new data, updating parameters in real time. This approach is particularly useful for applications like stock market prediction and real-time personalization, where immediate adjustments are necessary. A hybrid approach, combining periodic batch retraining with online learning, allows models to balance stability and adaptability.

Deploying updated models efficiently is another critical aspect of continuous learning. Organizations must ensure that new models are rigorously tested before deployment to avoid introducing errors or unintended biases. A/B testing is a widely used technique that allows organizations to compare the performance of a new model against the existing one in a controlled environment. If the updated model demonstrates superior performance, it can be promoted to full production. Alternatively, canary deployments involve rolling out the new model to a small subset of users before a wider release, allowing for gradual validation and risk mitigation.

Automation plays a key role in ensuring that model maintenance processes are scalable and efficient. MLOps (Machine Learning Operations) practices integrate machine learning workflows with DevOps principles, enabling seamless automation of model training, testing, and deployment. Tools like Kubeflow, MLflow, and TensorFlow Extended (TFX) help manage the entire machine learning lifecycle, from data ingestion and preprocessing to model versioning and deployment. By implementing automated pipelines, organizations can reduce manual intervention, streamline model updates, and minimize downtime.

In addition to retraining and deployment, interpretability and explainability remain essential considerations in continuous learning. As models evolve, their decision-making processes should remain transparent and understandable to stakeholders. Explainable AI techniques, such as SHAP (Shapley Additive Explanations) and LIME (Local Interpretable Model-agnostic Explanations), provide insights into how models arrive at their predictions. Ensuring transparency is particularly important in regulated industries such as finance and healthcare, where decision-making accountability is crucial.

Ultimately, continuous learning and model maintenance are not just technical necessities but strategic imperatives for organizations leveraging AI. Without ongoing adaptation, machine learning models risk becoming obsolete, leading to suboptimal business decisions and eroded user trust. By implementing proactive monitoring, efficient data pipeline management, adaptive retraining strategies, automated deployment workflows, and robust interpretability measures, organizations can ensure that their AI systems remain accurate, resilient, and aligned with real-world changes. In a rapidly evolving technological landscape, the ability to continuously learn and improve is what distinguishes successful AI-driven enterprises from those that struggle to keep pace.

Challenges in Maintaining Machine Learning Models

Machine learning models are dynamic systems that operate in constantly evolving environments. Once deployed, they interact with real-world data, user behaviors, and changing external conditions, all of which can significantly impact their effectiveness. If not continuously monitored and updated, models can degrade over time, leading to reduced accuracy, biased predictions, and poor decision-making. Maintaining machine learning models in production is an ongoing challenge that involves identifying and addressing various forms of data and model drift, managing computational and infrastructure constraints, and ensuring that models remain interpretable and trustworthy.

One of the most critical challenges in maintaining machine learning models is concept drift, which occurs when the statistical relationship between input features and the target variable changes. Concept drift can arise in a variety of domains where the underlying patterns governing the data evolve over time. For example, in financial fraud detection, fraudsters continuously adapt their methods to bypass security measures. A model trained on past fraud patterns may fail to recognize new attack strategies, leading to undetected fraudulent transactions. Concept drift can be categorized into different types based on how it manifests in the data. Sudden drift occurs when there is an abrupt shift in the target distribution, such as when a change in government regulations immediately affects consumer lending policies. Gradual drift happens when the relationship between features and the target variable shifts incrementally over time, making it harder to detect until performance degradation becomes significant. Recurring drift follows predictable seasonal patterns, such as an increase in online shopping fraud during holiday seasons. To effectively manage concept drift, organizations need to implement continuous performance monitoring systems that track model accuracy and detect deviations from expected outcomes. Retraining pipelines should be designed to update models dynamically based on new data, and in some cases, adaptive learning techniques such as reinforcement learning or meta-learning may be employed to allow models to adjust automatically to changing conditions.

Another major issue in model maintenance is data drift, also known as covariate shift, which occurs when the distribution of input features changes over time while the relationship between inputs and outputs remains unchanged. In real-world applications, data drift can be caused by various factors, including market trends, changes in user behavior, or external influences such as economic downturns or global pandemics. For instance, an e-commerce recommendation system trained in past purchase behaviors may become ineffective if consumer preferences shift due to changes in product availability or emerging fashion trends. Data drift can lead to situations where the model's assumptions about the data no longer hold, causing performance degradation even if the model's internal logic remains sound. Detecting data drift requires statistical analysis techniques such as Kolmogorov-Smirnov tests or population stability index (PSI) measurements, which compare the distribution of incoming data to historical training data. Once detected, data drift can be mitigated by updating training datasets, incorporating active learning strategies where models request human-labeled data for uncertain predictions, or using drift-aware model architectures that adapt to distributional changes.

Label drift is another challenge in maintaining machine learning models, particularly in applications that rely on human-annotated labels. Label distributions can shift over time due to changes in human perception, evolving definitions of concepts, or biases introduced during annotation. This is especially relevant in fields like sentiment analysis, where the way people express emotions changes over time. A sentiment classifier trained in text data from five years ago may misinterpret modern slang, emojis, or context shifts in language. In the legal industry, changes in case law and judicial interpretations can render older annotations obsolete, requiring continuous updates to labeled datasets. Addressing label drift requires ongoing validation of model outputs, re-annotation efforts, and the use of semi-supervised learning techniques where the model learns from both labeled and unlabeled data while incorporating human feedback.

Model staleness and degradation occur when a previously well-performing model becomes less effective due to shifts in real-world conditions. This issue is particularly prominent in high-stakes applications like healthcare, finance, and cybersecurity. For example, a credit risk model that was trained on economic conditions from five years ago may not reflect recent changes in inflation, employment rates, or consumer spending behavior, leading to incorrect risk assessments. Similarly, in healthcare, machine learning models used for disease prediction must incorporate the latest medical research findings and treatment protocols to ensure accuracy. Unlike concept drift and data drift, which involve changes in data distributions, model staleness is a broader issue that encompasses changes in external conditions that the model was not designed to handle. To address this, organizations must establish regular model audits, schedule periodic retraining, and implement online learning approaches where models continuously learn from new data without requiring full retraining.

Scalability and performance issues add another layer of complexity to maintaining machine learning models in production. As data volumes increase, the computational cost of retraining and serving models grows, potentially making frequent updates infeasible. In applications like social media content recommendation, financial forecasting, or autonomous driving, machine learning models must process vast amounts of data in real-time while maintaining low-latency responses. Traditional batch retraining approaches may not be scalable due to the sheer volume of incoming data. Instead, organizations need to implement incremental learning techniques, where models are updated with new data without being retrained from scratch. Federated learning can also be employed in scenarios where training data is distributed across multiple devices, allowing models to learn collaboratively without centralizing all data. Additionally, optimizing model architectures through techniques like quantization, pruning, and knowledge distillation can help reduce computational overhead while maintaining high performance.

Ensuring interpretability and trust in machine learning models is another crucial aspect of long-term model maintenance. In regulated industries such as healthcare and finance, black-box models that provide highly accurate predictions but lack transparency can be problematic. Stakeholders, including regulators, customers, and internal decision-makers, need to understand how a model arrives at its conclusions. Explainability techniques such as SHAP (Shapley Additive Explanations), LIME (Local Interpretable Model-agnostic Explanations), and counterfactual analysis help provide insights into model predictions, making it easier to diagnose performance issues and address biases. Additionally, model documentation frameworks like Google's Model Cards and Datasheets for Datasets help standardize information about how models were trained, evaluated, and deployed, improving transparency and accountability.

To address these challenges effectively, organizations must adopt a systematic approach that combines proactive monitoring, automated retraining pipelines, and scalable deployment strategies. Continuous integration and continuous deployment (CI/CD) workflows for machine learning, often referred to as MLOps, can help streamline model updates while minimizing disruptions. By integrating real-time performance tracking, anomaly detection, and rollback mechanisms, organizations can ensure that models are updated when necessary while maintaining stability. Automated A/B testing and canary deployments allow new model versions to be tested on a small subset of users before full-scale deployment, reducing the risk of unintended performance regressions. Additionally, human-in-the-loop (HITL) approaches, where machine learning models work alongside human experts who validate critical decisions, can further enhance reliability in high-stakes applications.

Ultimately, maintaining machine learning models in production requires a balance between stability and adaptability. While frequent updates help ensure that models remain relevant, excessive retraining can introduce unnecessary complexity and computational overhead. Organizations must strike a balance by implementing efficient model monitoring, designing retraining strategies based on empirical performance thresholds, and leveraging domain expertise to guide updates. In a rapidly changing world, the ability to sustain and improve machine learning models over time is critical to maximizing their long-term value, ensuring fairness, and maintaining trust among stakeholders.

Strategies for Continuous Learning and Model Maintenance

To address the challenges associated with maintaining machine learning models over time, organizations must adopt a structured approach to continuous learning and model maintenance. This involves implementing robust monitoring systems, automating retraining processes, optimizing model efficiency, and ensuring transparency in evolving models. A well-defined strategy ensures that machine learning models remain accurate, fair, and adaptable as they interact with dynamic real-world environments.

Continuous monitoring and performance tracking play a crucial role in identifying potential model degradation before it impacts decision-making. Real-time model monitoring allows organizations to track key performance metrics such as accuracy, precision, recall, and AUC-ROC, which help assess the reliability of predictions. Tools such as MLflow, TensorBoard, and WhyLabs provide visualization and logging capabilities that make it easier to analyze model behavior. Drift detection techniques are essential for recognizing changes in data distributions that can lead to reduced model performance. Statistical tests such as the Kolmogorov-Smirnov test and Jensen-Shannon divergence compare feature distributions between training and live data to identify significant shifts. In cases where labeled data is unavailable, unsupervised drift detection methods like autoencoders and clustering-based anomaly detection can highlight unusual changes in input data. Another approach involves training a secondary model specifically designed to predict whether new data belongs to the same distribution as the training data, providing an additional safeguard against unexpected data shifts.

Automated model retraining is another critical component of continuous learning. Instead of manually updating models, organizations can implement scheduled retraining, where models are periodically updated at fixed intervals, such as weekly or monthly, to incorporate new data. However, a more efficient approach is trigger-based retraining, which initiates model updates only when significant drift is detected. This ensures that retraining occurs only when necessary, balancing model freshness with computational efficiency. Online learning techniques enable models to update their parameters incrementally as new data arrives, rather than retraining from scratch.

Stochastic gradient descent (SGD) is commonly used in online learning settings to enable models to learn from a continuous stream of data while maintaining efficiency.

Active learning techniques enhance the efficiency of labeling efforts by prioritizing the most uncertain or impactful data points for human annotation. Instead of labeling an entire dataset, active learning identifies the samples that would provide the most value for improving model performance. This significantly reduces the cost and effort associated with data annotation while ensuring that the model learns from the most informative examples. Human-in-the-loop AI systems combine human expertise with automated learning, allowing experts to validate and refine model predictions in critical applications such as medical diagnosis and fraud detection. This approach ensures that machine learning models do not operate in isolation but benefit from human judgment, especially in cases where incorrect predictions could have serious consequences.

Managing multiple versions of machine learning models is essential for tracking model performance over time and ensuring that improvements are well-documented. Model versioning allows organizations to store different iterations of a model along with metadata that includes training data, hyperparameters, and evaluation metrics. Tools like Data Version Control (DVC) and MLflow facilitate version control by enabling teams to keep track of model changes and revert to previous versions when necessary. A/B testing and the champion-challenger approach provide mechanisms for deploying multiple versions of a model in production and comparing their performance on real-world data. A/B testing randomly assigns users to different model versions to determine which performs best, while the champion-challenger approach involves continuously testing a new "challenger" model against the current "champion" model to determine if an upgrade is warranted.

Optimizing machine learning models is necessary to ensure efficiency in deployment, especially in resource-constrained environments. Feature engineering updates involve periodically reevaluating feature importance and removing redundant or outdated features that no longer contribute to model accuracy. Feature selection techniques such as recursive feature elimination and SHAP-based importance ranking help identify the most relevant inputs. Model compression techniques like quantization, knowledge distillation, and pruning reduce computational complexity while preserving model accuracy. Quantization lowers the precision of numerical representations to make models more efficient for deployment on edge devices, while knowledge distillation involves training a smaller model (the "student") to mimic a larger, more complex model (the "teacher"), resulting in a lightweight model that retains most of the predictive power. Pruning removes unnecessary neurons or parameters from deep learning models, reducing memory usage and inference time without sacrificing significant performance. Hyperparameter optimization further enhances model performance by fine-tuning model parameters using automated search techniques such as Bayesian optimization, grid search, or evolutionary algorithms.

Implementing continuous integration and continuous deployment (CI/CD) pipelines for machine learning, commonly known as MLOps, streamlines the automation of training, validation, deployment, and monitoring processes. MLOps tools like Kubeflow, AWS SageMaker, and Google Vertex AI provide scalable frameworks for managing machine learning workflows in production environments. Canary deployments are the best practice in MLOps, where new model versions are initially rolled out to a small subset of users before being deployed at scale. This gradual deployment approach minimizes risks by allowing teams to monitor the model's performance in a controlled environment before full release. Automated rollback mechanisms ensure that if a newly deployed model performs worse than expected, it can be quickly replaced with the previous version without disrupting operations.

As machine learning models evolve, ensuring transparency and explainability is essential to maintain trust among users and regulatory bodies. Explainable AI (XAI) techniques such as SHAP (Shapley Additive Explanations) and LIME (Local Interpretable Model-Agnostic Explanations) help interpret how model decisions change over time. These methods provide insights into feature importance and decision-making processes, allowing stakeholders to understand why a model made a particular prediction. In high-impact domains such as healthcare and finance, regulatory frameworks such as the GDPR's "Right to Explanation" mandate that organizations provide clear justifications for automated decisions. Ensuring compliance with such regulations requires machine learning models to be designed with interpretability in mind, allowing affected individuals to contest decisions and request human intervention when necessary.

The combination of real-time monitoring, automated retraining, efficient labeling strategies, model optimization, CI/CD pipelines, and explainability techniques forms the foundation of a robust continuous learning and model maintenance strategy. By adopting these practices, organizations can ensure that their machine learning models remain accurate, efficient, and fair over time. Given the rapidly changing nature of data and business environments, sustaining high-performing models requires an ongoing commitment to adaptation, accountability, and transparency. The ability to proactively address model degradation, optimize resource utilization, and provide clear explanations for predictions will be key to building reliable and trustworthy AI systems that serve diverse users effectively.

Real-World Applications for Continuous Learning

Continuous learning is crucial in real-world applications where machine learning models must adapt to changing conditions, new data patterns, and evolving user behaviors. Without ongoing updates and maintenance, even the most advanced AI systems can become outdated, leading to decreased accuracy, poor decision-making, and potential harm. Several industries rely on continuous learning to ensure their AI-driven applications remain relevant, efficient, and effective.

Fraud detection in banking and financial services is one of the most dynamic applications of continuous learning. Fraudsters continuously develop new techniques to evade detection, making static models ineffective over time. Machine learning models used for fraud detection must constantly evolve to recognize emerging fraud patterns and differentiate between legitimate transactions and fraudulent ones. Banks and payment platforms leverage real-time monitoring systems that analyze vast amounts of transaction data to identify anomalies. When a potential fraudulent transaction is detected, feedback mechanisms allow investigators to validate the findings, and the model is subsequently retrained with the newly identified fraud patterns. Adaptive fraud detection systems use online learning techniques, updating their parameters as new fraudulent activities emerge without requiring complete retraining. This ensures that security measures remain robust and responsive to evolving threats while minimizing false positives that could disrupt legitimate transactions.

Recommendation systems used by streaming platforms, e-commerce websites, and social media networks heavily depend on continuous learning to provide personalized experiences to users. Platforms like Netflix and Spotify update their recommendation algorithms based on user interactions, preferences, and content trends. When a user engages with specific types of content, machine learning models analyze these interactions in real time and adjust future recommendations accordingly. Without continuous learning, these systems would quickly become ineffective, as they would fail to capture shifts in user preferences, seasonal trends, and emerging content categories. Advanced recommendation engines employ reinforcement learning techniques, where models iteratively refine their recommendations based on real-time feedback from users. This allows platforms to increase user engagement and satisfaction by continuously adapting to individual tastes and broader content consumption patterns.

Healthcare AI applications, such as disease prediction and diagnostic models, rely on continuous learning to incorporate new medical research, patient data, and emerging health trends. In hospitals and medical institutions, AI-driven diagnostic systems assist doctors in identifying diseases, predicting patient outcomes, and recommending treatments. However, medical knowledge evolves rapidly, with new research findings, treatment guidelines, and epidemiological data influencing clinical decisions. Continuous learning enables healthcare AI models to integrate these updates, ensuring they remain accurate and aligned with the latest scientific knowledge. For instance, predictive models used for detecting diseases such as cancer or heart conditions must be retrained regularly with new patient data to improve diagnostic accuracy. In the case of a global pandemic, AI models analyzing disease spread and predicting outbreaks must quickly adapt to real-time infection data, genetic mutations, and vaccine developments. Without continuous learning, outdated models could provide inaccurate diagnoses, leading to misinformed medical decisions and potentially harming patients.

Autonomous vehicles rely on continuous learning to navigate real-world environments safely. Self-driving cars operate in highly dynamic conditions where road layouts, traffic patterns, and environmental factors constantly change. Machine learning models used in autonomous driving systems process sensor data, such as camera feeds, LiDAR scans, and GPS signals, to make real-time driving decisions. These models must continuously learn from new experiences, including edge cases such as unusual weather conditions, unexpected pedestrian movements, and rare traffic scenarios. When an autonomous vehicle encounters a new driving situation, data from the event is logged and used to refine future decision-making processes. Fleet-wide learning enables multiple self-driving vehicles to share insights, allowing all vehicles in a network to benefit from collective experiences. Without continuous learning, self-driving systems would struggle to adapt to unforeseen scenarios, increasing the risk of accidents and making autonomous driving impractical in complex environments.

Across all these applications, continuous learning and model maintenance are essential to ensure AI systems remain relevant and effective. Machine learning models degrade over time if they are not regularly updated to reflect changes in data distributions and external conditions. Organizations must establish robust pipelines for monitoring model performance, detecting drift, and triggering retraining processes. Automated retraining strategies ensure that models remain aligned with evolving data without requiring manual intervention. Drift detection techniques allow organizations to identify when models start to deviate from expected behavior, prompting corrective actions before performance deteriorates significantly.

Human-in-the-loop feedback mechanisms play a crucial role in maintaining AI model quality, particularly in high-stakes applications like fraud detection, healthcare, and autonomous systems. By incorporating human expertise into the learning process, AI models can improve their decision-making capabilities while avoiding biases and errors that arise from fully automated systems. For example, fraud analysts reviewing flagged transactions can provide feedback to refine fraud detection models, doctors validating AI-assisted diagnoses can ensure medical models align with clinical best practices, and safety drivers monitoring autonomous vehicles can report anomalies that require model adjustments.

MLOps best practices, which integrate machine learning development with operational processes, provide the foundation for scalable and reliable AI deployment. Continuous integration and deployment (CI/CD) pipelines automate the process of training, testing, and deploying machine learning models. Organizations using MLOps tools such as Kubeflow, AWS SageMaker, and Google Vertex AI can streamline model maintenance, ensuring that updates are implemented efficiently while minimizing downtime. Version control for models allows teams to track changes, compare different model iterations, and revert to previous versions if necessary. Canary deployments and A/B testing enable organizations to roll out new model updates gradually, ensuring that performance improvements are validated before full-scale implementation.

As AI systems become increasingly embedded in critical decision-making processes, continuous learning is no longer optional but a necessity. Machine learning models must evolve alongside the data and environments they operate in to maintain accuracy and reliability. Without proactive monitoring and maintenance, even the most well-designed models will eventually become obsolete, leading to suboptimal outcomes and potential risks. Businesses and organizations that prioritize continuous learning can keep their AI systems relevant, adaptive, and effective in real-world scenarios, ensuring long-term success in a rapidly changing digital landscape.

"The true power of AI lies not just in its intelligence, but in its ability to continuously learn, adapt, and evolve alongside the ever-changing world. Without ongoing monitoring, retraining, and optimization, even the most advanced models become obsolete. By embracing continuous learning and ethical AI practices, we can ensure that machine learning systems remain relevant, reliable, and beneficial to society for years to come.

www.ingramcontent.com/pod-product-compliance
Ingram Content Group UK Ltd.
Pitfield, Milton Keynes, MK11 3LW, UK
UKHW042018290726
14061UKWH00001BB/62

9 782982 207028